"Required reading for anyone who hates being t... coming thing. Internet web-based TV/film series co... ever dreamed of building an entertainment empi... or investor.

Pyle peers behind the smoke and mirrors of rumor, opinion, and publicity to lay out chapter, verse, and schema for how tyros and professionals alike have built successful brands where cute videos of cats that look like Hitler end and real cash begins.

Using the most successful web series as his models, Pyle lays out a map for where the pitfalls can be found and where the winners landed to haul in jaw-dropping numbers. Don't go it alone. Take Marx Pyle with you."
— Victor Miller, writer of *Friday the 13th* and winner of 3 Emmys & 4 WGA awards

"Pyle brings his experience as both an indie filmmaker and web series producer to the table in order to create this book — a great tool for anyone with aspirations toward developing their own web series. I highly recommend it to anyone interested in web series as well as those looking to create their own web series and blaze their own trail."
— Ian Cullen, editor of *SciFiPulse* & host of *SFP-Now*

"An amazing resource for aspiring and veteran web creators. I wish this book existed when I started making web series! From concept to distribution and monetization, this book covers it all."
— Jeff Burns, creator of *Super Knocked Up* & *Super Geeked Up*, member of the Board of Directors of the International Academy of Web Television

"Pyle has not only given us an invaluable insight into the birth of the web series as a growing industry, but has also created a toolkit for building and launching a successful project. It is a battle-tested field manual for anyone looking to start their own show."
— Ben Bays, executive producer of the series *Aidan 5*

"Pyle sets the record straight for the web-curious by respecting this fantastic medium as its own unique beast, distinguishing it from the film and TV series formats we have all been living in for years."
— Nick & Candice, hosts of *Limited Release Podcast*

"Covers how to create and market a web series, but more importantly, 'why' and if this is the right format for you. Before you put your blood, sweat, and tears into your project, take the time to set yourself up for success."
— Tim Keaty, host of *Surfing Aliens*

"A must read for any filmmaker involved in this wonderful new frontier. It's direct, honest, and insightful."
— Jason Brasier, web series creator of Drifterseries.com

"Essential reading. This is the how-to guide for web series — from concept to final product — that nascent creators and artists have been waiting for."
— John Kenneth Muir, author of *Horror Films of the 1970s* and *Horror Films FAQ*

"I've read several books on producing web series, and they're all so broad and generic they're just pretending to be web-relevant. But Pyle's book covers Instagram, Twitter, crowd-funding, Google+, you name it. In an industry that changes daily, he somehow has managed to write about it in a style that doesn't feel a day behind."
— Chad Gervich, writer, producer; TV: *Wipeout, After Lately, Dog with a Blog*; Books: *How to Manage Your Agent; Small Screen, Big Picture*

Dedication

To Julie, who always believed in my crazy ideas.

MARX H. PYLE

TELEVISION on the
WILD, WILD WEB

And How To Blaze Your Own Trail

MICHAEL WIESE PRODUCTIONS

Published by Michael Wiese Productions
12400 Ventura Blvd. #1111
Studio City, CA 91604
(818) 379-8799, (818) 986-3408 (FAX)
mw@mwp.com
www.mwp.com

Cover design by Johnny Ink. www.johnnyink.com
Interior design by William Morosi
Edited by David Wright
Printed by McNaughton & Gunn

Manufactured in the United States of America

Library of Congress Cataloging-in-Publication Data

Pyle, Marx H., 1977-
 Television on the wild, wild web : and how to blaze your own trail / by Marx H. Pyle.
    pages cm
 ISBN 978-1-61593-199-6
 1. Television authorship. 2. Internet television. I. Title.
 PN1992.7.P95 2014
 808'.066791--dc23
                        20140189612

Printed on Recycled Stock

CONTENTS

CHAPTER 3

MONEY, PLEASE

CHAPTER 4

THE QUEST FOR TALENT

CHAPTER 5

SPREADING THE WORD 102

CHAPTER 6

THE MANY PATHS OF DISTRIBUTION 135

CHAPTER 7

CHAPTER 8

SPECIAL ACKNOWLEDGMENTS

This book wouldn't have been possible if not for the web-television and filmmaking talents that I have interviewed over the years, a few of which have become my friends (not just Facebook friends either). I know this is far from a complete list, but here are some of those brilliant talents who shared views that helped shape this book. I hope all continue to find success in this crazy new frontier of filmmaking:

Ben Bays, Vidas Barzdukas, Bryan Michael Block, Maya Sayre, Robb Padgett, Tanya Ihnen, Steven Lekowicz, Jeff Burns, Jourdan Gibson, Blake Calhoun, Joe Wilson, Jason Brasier, Brittney Greer, John Kenneth Muir, Ben Dobyns, Thomas Gofton, Anne Flournoy, Jen Page, Monte Cook, Mark Pezzula, Darren Chadwick-Hussein, Ed Robinson, Jodie Younse, Vanessa Verduga, Jonathan Robbins, Matthew Carvery, Leesa Dean, Sarah Moore, Jeff Moore, Justin Bondi, Andrew Ludington, Richard Cutting, Doug Jones, Scott Klein, Yuri Brown, Dan Williams, Chris Allen, Travis Gordon, Josh Bernhard, John Beck Hofmann, John Jackson, Michael Flores, Tony E. Valenzuela, Ken Whitman, Tim Gooch, Larry Elmore, Gabe Michael, Ryan Holloway, Jenni Powell, Paul Best, Laura Olson, Clancy Bundy, Adam Boyd, Jade Warpenburg, Peter D. Adkison, Thomas Koch, Chuck Marshall, Vanessa Leinani, Matt Vancil, John Cabrera, Kent Nichols, Chris Stone, Travis Richey, James Cawley, Rick Chambers, Mark Burchett, John Kelley, Charles Root, Barry Dodd, Stephanie Thorpe, Paula Rhodes, Victor Solis, Doug Drexler, Joanna Gaskell, Edwin Perez, Tara Pratt, Rob Hunt, Philip Cook, Mark Hyde, Rebekkah Johnson, Jerry Kokich, Steve Marra, Thomas Bannister, Justin Lutsky, Adam J. Cohen, Ron Newcomb, and many more....

WHO SHOULD READ THIS BOOK?

Let's be clear. This book is NOT for everyone. It is for a certain type of creator or team of people wanting to get their project out into the world. This could be...

1. **Film Students** who want to learn the craft of filmmaking for the web and to get their work in front of as many eyeballs as possible to help them take the next step in their young careers.

2. **Independent Filmmakers** who want to create the stories that they want to create, and want to find a fanbase online that will support their work.

3. **Web Series Creators** who live and breath the Internet and want to tell their stories on the Internet for the world to see.

4. **Veteran Filmmakers** looking for new ways to market or raise funds for their project. Perhaps they just need to re-evaluate the ways they make films to take advantage of new trends in filmmaking marketing and distribution.

5. **Crowdfunding Project Creators** who want to learn how to fund their projects with crowdfunding platforms like Kickstarter, Indiegogo, and others.

6. **Marketing Specialists** who want to better apply their skills for the entertainment industry.

7. Any **Business Professional** who needs funds for a project or to create awareness for it.

Leading up to this book I have done extensive research, interviewed over 90 web series creators, worked on multiple web series (*Reality On Demand, Aidan 5, Star Trek: Phase II, Book of Dallas*, etc.), and judged for the International Academy of Web Series Awards and The Geekie Awards. One thing I can tell you is that your budget does not define success, your creativity combined with knowledge rewards you with success. This book will give you the tools you need to blaze your own path on this new frontier, the wild, wild web we call the Internet.

FOREWORD

When Marx called me the other day, I got really excited. I was sure he was finally ready to go forward with my story idea of a killer robot sent back in time in a Delorean to stop a ragtag group of rebels from finding the Holy Grail before an evil empire can get its hands on it and take over the universe. Instead he told me about this new book he was writing about the web television revolution.

"Oh, so it's a book about *The Guild*," I said.

"Well, I talk about *The Guild*, but it's about all the amazing web series that are being made right now," Marx replied.

"Do they all star Felicia Day?"

"Um, no. Felicia Day is awesome but there are a plethora of phenomenal actors in the web television world."

"Oh cool. Are all these web series created by Joss Whedon? And did you just use the word 'plethora'?"

"I did. And no, there are hundreds of web series out there by a vast array of ridiculously talented creators. You have a web series too, Jeff."

"Holy crap! You're right, I do. Hey, can I write the Foreword?"

"Um ... yeah why not? Felicia Day and Joss Whedon already turned me down."

I'm sure Marx will tell you that's exactly how the conversation went. Or maybe not. In any case, I'm beyond thrilled to be writing the Foreword to a book that couldn't come at a better time and one I know will be amazingly helpful to both aspiring and veteran web series creators.

Being part of this exciting new web television movement has been the most rewarding thing I've done. It feels like we're among the pioneers of the next huge wave in entertainment. Much like television in the 1940s and 50s. And that's a pretty amazing feeling. And Marx is right about how many amazingly talented creators there are in the web space. But they're not only talented. They're also incredibly supportive. In all the things I've done and all the different areas of filmmaking I've been a part of, I've never seen a more supportive and amazing community than that of the web series.

And Marx has been a huge part of that community. Which is just one of many reasons he's the perfect person to write this book. He's made his own web series and produced and worked on several other series. He's talked with scores of web creators as part of his and his wife's super-cool podcast GenreTainment. So he not only brings his own knowledge and experience to the table, but also that of countless other web creators. And through GenreTainment, he's been promoting so many of us in the web space. With this combination of talent, experience, promotion, and the knowledge of others, it's hard to think of a better author for this book. He's like the Yoda of the web world. Which is exciting because that means I get to be Luke Skywalker! And I've always wanted to be a Jedi and wield a lightsaber (outside of the plastic one I have at home and use to attack evil Sith lords I come across on a daily basis).

I wish this book existed when I was making my web series. I would have bought it in a second. Marx takes you through every aspect of the process from coming up with a killer, marketable concept to casting, distribution, and monetization possibilities. Marx gives you everything you need to know to begin your journey into this "Wild West of the Web." And it's a journey I truly hope you join us on. I think you'll find it an inspiring and revolutionary one. Marx and I can't wait to welcome you into the ranks of the groundbreaking web creators exploring this new frontier.

I also wish the book told me how I could be transported into the world of *Star Trek* and explore the galaxy on the *Enterprise*. Maybe Marx will tackle that in his next book. Or you could go watch his awesome series *Reality on Demand*, which deals with that very scenario. And while you're at it, please check out all the other amazing series on the web right now that are breaking new ground, telling riveting stories, and entertaining so many people. I think you'll be impressed and inspired by how much web-based storytelling is flourishing.

Web series are the *future*. They're the *now*. Web series creators are producing the most original and story-driven content right now. I believe we're the future of entertainment.

And I have never felt more at home than when I entered the web series world and the community of web series creators. This is the world I want to keep working in. I've never been around a community that's more passionate, talented, supportive, and collaborative than the web series community. So I don't hesitate in the slightest in encouraging you to enter this amazing world and keep reading on. Becoming a web series creator is the best decision I've ever made (well, that and entering the Jedi Academy). I hope it becomes a decision many of you choose to do. And I can't wait to meet you and help each other and our community grow. Thanks so much for reading! Now you can get on to the real stuff from the amazing Marx Pyle. And big thanks to Marx for letting me write this Foreword. And to Felicia Day and Joss Whedon for being too busy to write it.

So, huge congrats to Marx on this awesome book and to you for taking the first step in joining the web series community. You've just joined the revolution!

• • •

Jeff Burns is the writer/director of the superhero web series *Super Knocked Up*, host of the geek pop culture show *Super Geeked Up*, and a member of the Board of Directors of the International Academy of Web Television.

INTRODUCTION: SIGN UP FOR THE REVOLUTION!

Web Television: Original television content produced for broadcast via the Internet. Part of this recently emerging medium are web series, a series of videos often in episodic form.

Are You Ready?

Are you ready to become a pioneer, blazing your own trail through the future of entertainment?

There is a revolution happening in entertainment and it is all the Internet's fault.

It's a revolution that is changing the rules for television and filmmaking and the major studios are scrambling to figure out their place in this new world. As writer/producer John Rodgers (*Leverage, Transformers*) once told me in an interview: "There is an old saying: no one wants to be alive during the revolution. Before the revolution and after the revolution are great. During the revolution sucks. We're 'during the revolution' right now and we just don't know where it's going to end."

A shift in the rules causes chaos as everyone tries to figure out how to make it work. But there are solid guidelines and examples of what is working and what is not working. My hope is that my interviews with over 90 web series creators and my own experience working on web series (*Reality On Demand, Aidan 5, Star Trek: Phase II, Book of Dallas,* and more) will provide clear information and tips on helping you join the revolution and be successful.

Making a web series is actually only a fraction of the work. About 70% of the work kicks in after you make your web series. To be heard in this ever-growing ocean of web television content, you'll need a loud and unique voice. Don't believe me?

To give you a better idea of the growing number of web series each year and the increasing production quality, let's take a look at the statistics from the International Academy of Web Television (IAWTV) awards. They had a total of 473 web series submitted to the 2013 IAWTV Awards, which is a 76% increase in the number of web series from the previous year. Their numbers also show that the value of original web series productions in 2012 is over $135 million, versus 2011 when the industry was valued at $45 million.

Now, keep in mind that the IAWTV Awards do not represent every web series out there. There are still many independent and studio-owned web series that didn't submit. But that still gives you a good idea of the overall growth in the number of shows out there. So how do you expect to compete?

Read this book and you'll learn how. I put it all in clear language that anyone can understand. Throughout you'll find checklists, references, and resources for further exploration. This book is the book I wish I had when trekking from the world of indie film into the world of web television.

But first, let's start with what exactly this revolution is and how it is developing.

Ever since film has existed there have been independent film-makers. But there have been three huge obstacles for indie creators: production costs, funding, and distribution. But technology has finally provided ways around these hindrances.

In the '90s, a revolution started in independent film, with digital film equipment that gave rise to filmmakers like Kevin Smith and Robert Rodriguez. Little did we know, however, that it would pale in comparison to what would come with advances in the Internet. Not only has high definition video finally gotten to the point where it has been accepted as an equal to film with far less cost (well ... accepted by almost everyone), but the Internet offers an independent way to overcome the last two costly obstructions: distribution and funding. With the development of the Internet, we gained a cheap way to communicate video and build communities.

For so long, the way to get your film shown was a drawn-out process of paying for the possibility of having your film screened at a film festival and dreaming of a distributor discovering you. Usually, this dream involved being discovered at Sundance, where you were offered the perfect deal, making you rich and famous. In reality, this almost never happens. All too often, if the deal offers did come, the filmmaker would see little profit and lose control of their intellectual property. This is the unfortunate reality of independent film. Yes, there are the *Paranormal Activity* and *Blair Witch Project* indie hits, but let's look at the numbers. The Writers Guild of America reports an average of 50,000 screenplays are registered annually. We know only a fraction of these ever get funding to be made, and far fewer are ever seen by the general public. (In 2011, 610 films were released domestically.) Chances of making a substantial profit are very small. And, just to add insult to injury, this old, inefficient model is only getting more difficult with each year, as financial woes have caused studios to buy fewer independent productions and even fewer investors want to take a financial risk. Holding onto the old ways, which are themselves gasping to stay afloat, is even riskier than before. This makes the move to web television very tempting for filmmakers. Web series have become the new short film, creating opportunities for new filmmakers and acting as excellent starting points for a career in filmmaking.

It reminds me of when I interviewed Jamin Winans, writer/director of the indie cult film *Ink*. He was frustrated with his first feature, which got one of those standard distribution deals in which he never saw a dime. So, after premiering his next film, *Ink,* at Santa Barbara International Film Festival, he took on the Herculean task of having a run at film festivals and independent movie houses across the United States. Although successful in its own way, the film didn't really take off until someone copied a DVD onto a peer-to-peer network. Suddenly, it found widespread fans online.

"We did a self-release of *Ink* on DVD and within a day or two of the DVD coming out, someone had bit-torrented it. Before we knew it, *Ink* exploded on Pirate Bay. Our immediate reaction was shock, then joy," said Winans. "I think we realized that *Ink* was getting incredible exposure that we couldn't have possibly paid for. Consequently, our DVD sales increased as a result and a lot of very cool people have given us donations to help support the film."

This is an example of free downloads actually helping springboard a career. Not only did it cause an almost unknown film to take off in DVD sales, but it helped them get picked up for a very successful run on Hulu. If not for the Internet, Winans would likely have either given up filmmaking at some point or would still be making low budget films in Detroit. Instead, when I spoke to him not long after *Ink* took off, he was working on a project in Eastern Europe.

It's a good example of how filmmaking distribution is changing. The old way was hard and honestly only worked for a lucky, talented, and well-connected few. And don't get me started on trying to make an independent television series ... *a television series*??? Independent films have been made as long as films have been around, but no one made independent, low budget television. Even if you could afford to make multiple episodes, how in the world would you get it to an audience? Most film festivals wouldn't be interested and traditional television might stick you on public access, if you were lucky. But since 2004, independent television has taken off with early hits like Felicia Day's *The Guild* and *Star Trek: New Voyages* (which later would become known as *Star Trek: Phase II*). As the speeds of the Internet increased—becoming more High Definition-friendly—and the cost of cameras dropped, the number of new shows and the production quality of the shows have grown quickly. Now, there have been web series with budgets like $4.5 million CDN (Damian Kindler's *Sanctuary*), $6 million US (from *CSI* creator Anthony E. Zuiker's *Cybergeddon*), and $2 million US (Tom Hank's *Electric City*). But with Netflix jumping into original programming, with shows like *House of Cards* and *Hemlock Grove*, the waters have been stirred even more. Netflix's *House of Cards* with its all-star cast costs an estimated $50 million per 13-episode season. Plus, there is a growing community of web series creators forming different groups and award shows. But don't worry, this book will help you navigate through the waters of this ocean called web television.

What to Expect From This Book

Before we go any further, let's take a look at what you can expect from this book.

Chapter 1: The Perfect Brainstorm — Learning how to make your series stand out among the seemingly infinite shows on the web starts before you even write the script. It all starts here: brainstorming the perfect concept for a series. But wait! This isn't just about getting all artsy and coming up with imaginative, new stories. We also have to figure out if your story would make a good web series or if it would better flourish in some other format. I'll also show you how to figure out your audience and build a strong brand. Have some fun and play "Marx's Random Brainstorming Game" to help get the creative juices flowing.

Chapter 2: Building the Perfect Series — Now that we have the overall concept and brand figured out, it's time to build the blueprint of your series. What is a good length for a web series? What about each webisode? Can it be too short or too long? I break it down by genres and explain what type of story structures are best for each circumstance. This chapter offers some solid tips on writing, as well as unique ideas to think about when structuring a web series.

Chapter 3: Money, Please — Before you can start filming, you need to figure out how you are going to pay for your series. You can't make a high quality series on just your credit card ... well you could, but I wouldn't suggest it. I'll show you how to estimate your budget and the best options for funding.

Chapter 4: The Quest for Talent — Your series will only be as good as the people you have in front of the camera and behind the screen. I'll show you how to find good actors and crew. If you want the best of the best, you'll need to understand new media contracts. In this chapter, I remove the mystery of how to deal with the Screen Actors Guild and the Writers Guild of America.

Chapter 5: Spreading the Word — You've made the greatest series in the world! (At least that's what your mom says.) Now, how do your potential, devoted fans learn it exists? I share solid tips, both online and offline, to make your series stand out in the crowd.

Chapter 6: The Many Paths of Distribution — How do you make a profit? This question has challenged every show, even those backed by big studios. After I show you all of the options, you will understand which are the most successful choices for your series. YouTube, Hulu, Blip, Koldcast, etc. How should you put your web series online? Find out what platforms are on the web, along with the pros and cons of using each.

Chapter 7: Awards, Please? — Festivals aren't just for films anymore. Find out what web series festivals are out there, which other festivals are web series-friendly, and all of the major award shows that accept web television submissions.

Chapter 8: That's a Wrap! Now Let's Do It Again — Should you make a Season 2, a spin-off, a different web series, or call it quits? Did you succeed or not? Plus, I give you a long list of resources that will become your lifeline, including how to contact me for further assistance.

For a foundation on how to make a web series, especially during the production phase, check out the excellent *Byte-sized Television* written by Ross Brown. In *Television on the Wild, Wild Web*, I go into greater detail on what you do after the web series is actually filmed: marketing, funding, distribution, monetization (a.k.a. making money), and more. But some of these things require planning well before you film a single frame. So, we also look into building your brand and making sure your series concept will find an audience. And don't forget, you need to come up with a realistic budget and then figure out how you are going to raise the funds to (hopefully!) make your masterpiece. Remember, everyone has to find their own path to success, but this book will give you all the information you need on how to find yours. I've used research, my own experiences, and the advice of over 90 web series creators to develop this guide that demystifies this new frontier of web television. So, get to reading already ... oh ... and welcome to the Wild, Wild Web!

CHAPTER 1

THE PERFECT BRAINSTORM

"It seems obvious but the best advice I can give is to just go out and do something. Don't wait. Don't make excuses. Don't wait 'til you're 'ready,' because you'll never feel like you're ready. And it took me a long time to realize what that actually meant." — Josh Bernhard, writer/co-creator *Pioneer One*

For your show to have any level of success, you have to come up with a good marketing plan from the very start. If you have some money to spend and just want to make a project that looks nice for your reel or you have a story that you "must tell," then maybe this chapter isn't as important to you. But most likely, you want this project to do well. You want it to be seen by as many viewers as possible and you want it to make money, or at least create an opportunity that makes you money.

If that is the case, then this chapter is crucial. You must develop your concept so it can work in the format of a web series. You must learn what the current web television community is like, the major players and successful shows that exist. Walking in blind is one of the most common mistakes of a new web series creator. You'll be shocked how many first-time web series creators have watched only a handful of web series ... some have never even watched a single one. Could you imagine writing a TV pilot, but never watching a single episode of TV? Crazy, right? Well, a web series is more than just TV on the web. It has many unique elements that you must learn and an entirely different culture of creators. Don't reinvent the wheel. Learn the medium of web television before you make a single episode of your show.

COMMON MISTAKE: Making a web series without knowing what makes a web series unique.

Will History Repeat Itself?

If you are going to have any chance at being successful in web television, you need to know what the current web television community is like and how it got there. I know, I know ... history? ... snore... don't worry, this won't be a boring history lesson. I'm going to make it fun and give commentary on why each thing I mention is important and what chapters elaborate more on the subject matter. Plus, for you trivia nerds out there, I'll give you some nice trivia bits to add to the experience.

Here is a brief overview of the major points in web television history (with a few key points in film and TV history used for reference):

1800's – 1920's: The Birth of Film

The very foundation of film is based around a visual phenomenon, the illusion of movement created by a series of individual still pictures set into motion. It's a phenomenon that would eventually be dubbed persistence of vision, a concept first described scientifically and named by British physician Peter Mark Roget in 1824. So began the first big step for filmmaking.

The concept would spawn many devices trying to make use of the phenomenon: Thaumatrope, Fantascope, Zoetrope, Kinematoscope, and many more. But let's fast forward to May 20, 1895, the first motion picture to be screened before a paying audience. *Young Griffo v. Battling Charles Barnett* was shown in New York and consisted of a staged boxing match. Do you think Auguste and Louis Lumiere had any clue where this was going? The next year, Thomas Edison shoots *The Kiss*, the first kiss in film history ... scandalous!

In 1906 things get more "animated" when the first animated cartoon was produced, *Humorous Phases of Funny Faces*. By 1909 there are an estimated 9,000 movie theaters in the United States, a number which would only continue to grow. And by 1922, we get the early version of the visual trick that is all the rage today... 3D. On September 27, 1922, *The Power of Love* premiered at the Ambassador Hotel Theater in Los Angeles, making it the earliest confirmed 3D film shown to a paying audience.

1927 – The Silence Ends

Up until now, films have been silent, but that all changed with the first feature film presented as a "talkie," Warner Brothers' *The Jazz Singer*. It didn't take long for the talkie trend to catch on with audiences, and by the end of 1929, Hollywood movies were almost all talkies.

1920's – 1990's: The Growth of Home Entertainment

Meanwhile, while theatrical films get more elaborate in their technology, we start getting entertainment options at home. The concept of television had been around since the 1800s, but in 1927 it was a 21-year-old named Philo Farnsworth that produced the first electronic television picture. In the 1930s, experimental, and, yes, fuzzy broadcast television begins. In 1937, NBC TV studios is introduced, followed mere months later by the new CBS TV studios.

In the 1950s, we finally start to see the start of color television being introduced in the United States. (The first national colorcast was January 1, 1954, the Tournament of Roses Parade.) However, it would not be until the late '60s and early '70s until color television sets would become standard. And up until 1964, original movies were created for the movie theaters when the first made-for-TV film, *See How They Run,* is broadcast on NBC.

Sadly, up to this point, the ability to record your favorite TV programs isn't possible, but that changes in 1975 when Sony introduces Betamax (costing $2,295), the first videocassette recorder for home use. It would have competition though. On August 23, 1977, the United States received its first VHS-based VCR.

Meanwhile, cable is born. In 1972, HBO is the first cable network to be delivered nationwide by satellite transmission. And in 1976, the first basic cable network, Ted Turner's WTCG in Atlanta, is launched via satellite. Needless to say, the cable channels would grow at a lightning pace over the next few decades with news channels, music videos, reality TV, and more niche-specific channels.

1988 – The Neanderthal of the Web Series

In 1988, the Internet was moving at a snail's pace compared to what we are used to now. It was far from a mainstream hit with the public, yet we can trace the ancestry of the web series to this very year.

This was the year that "QuantumLink Serial" premiered on AOL. Many consider this to be the first episodic online story. Now this wasn't a web series per say, because there was no video, but it is the first attempt at episodic storytelling on the web. It was played out in online chat rooms, emails, and traditional narrative. After each week's chapter was published, users wrote to author Tracy Reed, suggesting how they could be part of the story. Each week, Reed chose one or more users and wrote them into the narrative, altering story lines to reflect readers' input for their unique "guest star appearances."

It was an interesting episodic storytelling method: Not just using the Internet to share a story, but also using it to interact with readers and actually let them influence the story. This basic concept would be explored further in future web series (see Chapter 6).

1995 – 1997: The Birth of the Modern Web Series, Netflix & DVDs

Web series would take a big step forward in 1995 when *The Spot*, created by Scott Zakarin, went online. It was the first advertiser-supported web series, and introduced the inclusion of photography and video.

Meanwhile, in other media, the DVD made its debut.

TRIVIA ALERT: First movie released on DVD was *Twister* on March 26, 1996.

On August 29, 1997, Netflix launches online, giving us an alternative to the more traditional pay-per-rental model in video rental stores. With Netflix, we can pick what we want online and have the DVD mailed to us. But this would be just the beginning of the powerhouse that Netflix would become.

2003 – 2004: The First Viral Web Series & Hit Fan Productions

Original web series were still far and few between and there hadn't been that many big hits yet with online users. But 2003 would usher in a new level of production value for live-action and animated web series.

On April 1, 2003, Rooster Teeth Productions released *Red vs. Blue* online and it became one of the most popular and longest running machinima series ever. It is often credited with helping machinima (animation by using 3D graphics, often from already existing video games) gain a mainstream audience.

January of 2004 would bring to the Internet one of the long running *Star Trek: The Original Series* fan productions called *Star Trek: New Voyages* (later renamed *Star Trek: Phase II*). The fan-made series is still active a decade after its debut, with episodes slated for a 2014 release. The series has had a number of guest stars, including *Star Trek* alumni Walter Koenig, George Takei, Grace Lee Whitney, Denise Crosby, D.C. Fontana, David Gerrold, Jon Povill, Norman Spinrad, George Clayton Johnson, Majel Barrett Roddenberry, and Eugene Roddenberry, Jr. It won the 2007 On-Line TV Guide Award for Best SciFi Webseries and has been nominated for Hugo and Nebula awards. It would be one of the first such fan-production web series (but far from the last) with dozens to follow in the settings of *Star Trek*, *Doctor Who*, *Star Wars*, and more.

So, we now see a growth in scripted web series, albeit most of it essentially fan productions. Although there were new video platforms popping up almost monthly, it wouldn't be until 2005 that video platforms would truly take off and original scripted web series would gain in popularity. What video platform jump-started this shift? I'll give you a hint ... it starts with a Y.

2005 – 2006: The Rise of YouTube and Death of VHS

An activation of a domain name would usher in a huge change in web television. On February 14th, 2005, the domain name YouTube.com is activated. On April 23, the first YouTube video is uploaded. It is a simple video called *Me at the Zoo* and shows co-founder Jawed Karim at the San Diego Zoo.

Although home videos and cat videos would be all the rage, it was just a matter of time until new and existing scripted web series found their home there. On August 1, the executive producers of *The Spot*, Todd Fisher and Stewart St. John (TV writers with credits including *The Incredible Hulk*; *The Mighty Morphin Power Rangers*; and *Sabrina, the Animated Series*), make their web series return with *California Heaven*. It is considered the first scripted TV series produced for online audiences.

In November, the web series *Ask A Ninja* premieres online and quickly becomes one of the most popular and profitable web series at the time. But it wouldn't take long for more original web series to appear online to give it competition.

Fast forward a few months to June, 2006, and arguably the most famous online series of the year, *lonelygirl15*, premieres on YouTube with a video blogger posing as a real 16-year-old using the username "lonelygirl." At first, the videos seemed to cover everyday normal events, but quickly became more bizarre involving secret occult practices and the disappearance of her parents. *Los Angeles Times* reporter Richard Rushfield was the first to provide proof of a hoax. Eventually, 16-year-old "Bree" was revealed to be played by 19-year-old actress Jessica Rose.

Two months later, another viral web series launched. *Sam Has 7 Friends*, an experiment by a group of young Los Angeles–based filmmakers, premiered on YouTube, iTunes, and Revver. The soap opera/murder mystery series has the compelling logline of: "Samantha Breslow has seven friends. On December 15, 2006, one of them will kill her." The series ran for 80 episodes and was most popular on iTunes, managing at times 10,000 downloads a day during the initial run of the series. While these were impressive numbers at the time, they would eventually be dwarfed by future popular web series.

Before we move on to the next few years, let's check in on the other mediums out there. Two new formats, HD DVD and Blu-ray Disc, are released commercially as the successor to DVD. HD DVD would lose the format war and be discontinued in 2008.

TRIVIA ALERT: In 2006, the last major Hollywood movie is released on VHS, *A History of Violence*.

2007 – 2008: The First Hit Web Series, New Video Platforms, and The Writers Strike

OK, so far we have popular fan productions, machinima, sketch comedies, and experimental viral videos. And YouTube and iTunes are the major platform options out there. But 2007 would start to change things. This year marks a big jump in popularity for original script content, some heavy money being invested in web television, and new video platform options.

On March 14, the Canadian science fiction series *Sanctuary* premieres online. It is created by Damian Kindler (*Stargate SG-1*) and stars Amanda Tapping (*Stargate SG-1*). At $4.5 million CND, it is easily the most expensive web series up to this point.

On July 27th, Felicia Day's *The Guild* premieres on YouTube. For Season 2, Microsoft makes an exclusive distribution deal for the series. Easily considered by most to be one of the first big scripted web series hits, it is one of the longest running web series. It lasted for six seasons and would eventually lead to Felicia Day starting her own YouTube channel, Geek & Sundry.

This year also led to new video platforms. On April 17, Will Ferrell launched the website FunnyorDie.com with the first video, *The Landlord*. And in July, Sony bought the Web video aggregator site called Grouper.com and renamed it Crackle.com to showcase both shows from their own library and original content.

Also this year, ABC.com makes it possible to play full episodes of their shows on their Web site. And remember Netflix? This is the year they begin to move away from its traditional model of mailing DVDs and introduce video-on-demand via the Internet.

The last big thing I want to mention for 2007, which would greatly effect the entire entrainment industry for the rest of the year and into 2008, was the Writers Guild of America strike. On November 5th, the strike began. Many writers have said publicly that the strike inspired them to create original content on the web, but more on that in a moment.

2008 starts with a great new funding option that will be used to help fund many a web series. In January, the international crowd-funding site Indiegogo is founded. See Chapter 3 to learn more about how you can use crowdfunding for your show.

On March 12th, we get a new major video platform player. Hulu launches for public access in the United States. And on the new web series front: on May 1, the first official video of the *Fred* series, *Fred on May Day,* was released on YouTube. It would quickly grow in popularity and be the first YouTube channel to have over one million subscribers.

The next big web series would soon follow. On July 15, Joss Whedon's *Dr. Horrible's Sing-Along Blog* premiered online with such huge numbers that it crashed its host's servers. Whedon, best known for creating *Buffy the Vampire Slayer* and *Firefly,* is quoted as saying the writer's strike inspired him to make this project.

On August 18th, the American science fiction web series *Gemini Division* premiered online. It starred Rosario Dawson (*Afterworld*) and aired on NBC.com as part of their online content. In a similar move of traditional network channels hosting online content, *Children's Hospital* premiered online at WB.com on December 8th. And on October 3rd, *Sanctuary* made the move from an eight-episode web series to premiering on television in both Canada and the United States. It's one of the earliest web series to make the move to traditional television and would live on for four seasons on TV.

On October 28th, the Internet television web site Strike.TV launched directly in response to the writer's strike. It featured several shows from various genres by well-known writers. Speaking of experienced TV talent moving into the web television community, on September 22nd Lisa Kudrow (*Friends*) created and starred in her web series *Web Therapy*.

So far, we've had original web series, original web series moving to traditional TV, and fan productions. But 2008 would also mark a huge spike in companion web series. Shows that are companion pieces to their traditional television counterparts began to premiere online. Examples from this year are web series of *The Office*, *Dexter*, *Weeds*, *Battlestar Galactica*, and *30 Rock*.

To date, many of the shows discussed have been self-funded or worked with more traditional studios, but 2008 is the year of one of the first branded series to find success. It is an IKEA-sponsored show, starring actress Illeana Douglass, called *Easy to Assemble*. We'll talk more about branded series in Chapter 3.

2009 – 2010: Web Television Gets Organized

Up to this point, makers of web series were all very independent and only those that crossed paths in person or on an online forum would really talk to each other. There was no real unifying organization for creators, that is until The International Academy of Web Television (IAWTV) was founded in December 2008. The nonprofit organization was founded in part to help organize the first major awards solely for the web television industry, the Streamy Awards. On March 28 2009, in collaboration with the IAWTV and the website Tubefilter, the Streamy Awards premiered online. Soon after, on October 19th, 2009, there was an inaugural meeting in Santa Monica, California, for the IAWTV. The estimated membership started at 100 and included Felicia Day as one of the board members (see, she is everywhere).

Another major milestone happened in 2009 that would help remove the funding obstacle for independent filmmakers of series and films: the founding of Kickstarter. In April 28, Kickstarter is founded and quickly becomes one of the most popular crowdfunding sites (see Chapter 3).

Unfortunately, the double rainbow of happy unity over the IAWTV and the Streamy's would fall apart in 2010. On April 11th, the 2nd Annual Streamy Awards, hosted by actor/comedian Paul

Scheer, was streamed live online from the Orpheum Theatre in Los Angeles, California. Due to technical problems, lewd jokes, and interruptions (including two streakers... yes, I'm not kidding), the award show gained many negative reviews from audience members and sponsors.

This prompts pressure from IAWTV members to distance themselves from the Streamy Awards, which the organization officially does do that year (although the controversy over the show is not cited as the reason for the parting), with plans to start their own award show. Also on October 5th, 2010, the newly formed IAWTV Board of Directors approves changes to make membership more inclusive rather than exclusive. Previously, IAWTV members were hand-selected by a committee of industry professionals. Going forward, people who are passionate about the web television and digital entertainment industries and can reasonably demonstrate they are working in online entertainment can join. Both steps are seen by outside critics as positive moves.

Some other big steps in the industry in 2010 included a Fred movie, called *Fred: The Movie*, which premiered on Nickelodeon with a rating of 7.6 million viewers on September 18th. A very successful adaptation of a web series to traditional TV. Also, on November 10th we saw a big change in Hulu. Up to this point you could watch anything on Hulu for free, but that changed with the launch of Hulu Plus, a monthly subscription service version. There are plenty of skeptics doubting that people would want to pay for Hulu. In little more than a year the number of paying subscribers reaches 1.5 million proving that viewers are open to paying for additional content.

2011 – present: Hollywood Jumps Into Original Web Series and Indie Funding Jumps

To continue the trend of growth for Hulu and Netflix, we saw on January 17th, 2011, Hulu streaming its first in-house production web series, the pop-culture news show "The Morning After." It would be followed by many other new original shows on Hulu. Meanwhile, in March 2011, Netflix announced plans to begin acquiring original content, beginning with the hour-long political drama "House of Cards," which debuted on the streaming service in early 2013. The series is helmed by David Fincher and star Kevin Spacey, with an estimated $50 million budget per 13-episode season.

The year 2011 was also a big year for YouTube. Google invests $100 million into a slate of over 100 newly funded original channels on YouTube. This leads to a shift from single-creator YouTube channels into new multi-channel networks (see Chapter 7), one of which is Geek & Sundry, founded by Felicia Day (there's that name again). In 2013 we see the first YouTube channel to surpass seven million channel subscribers. That honor goes to Smosh and it is a safe bet it will be followed by many more channels very soon.

But not everyone is happy with these new multi-channel networks at YouTube. In 2012 and 2013, a number of high-profile YouTube creators leave studios, very publicly complaining of unfair contracts creating comparisons in the media between YouTube networks and the exploitative Hollywood studios of the 1930s and '40s of Vaudeville (see how handy these history lessons can be).

Up to this point most web premieres were series or sketch comedy formats. Very few movies were premiering online first, but that changed on March 11th, 2011, when writer/director Sebastián Gutiérrez's (*Snakes on a Plane*) crime comedy *Girl Walks into a Bar* premiered on YouTube. The movie starred the likes of Carla Gugino, Rosario Dawson, Robert Forster, Danny DeVito, Josh Hartnett and Alexis Bledel, among others. It was the first time a major feature film was created exclusively for web distribution in the United States. It had a corporate sponsor for its release and on its opening weekend was watched by 250,000 YouTube users.

Warner Brothers also invested in more web content with their April 11th premiere on YouTube of *Mortal Kombat: Legacy*, produced by Warner Brothers Digital Distribution. At 5.5 million views it was YouTube's most viewed video for that week. Its success ensured more Warner Brothers web series in the future and more web series based on video games, including the Bryan Singer (*X-Men*)-produced series, *H+: The Digital Series*. It premiered on YouTube on August 8, 2012, and was also distributed by Warner Brothers Digital Distribution.

In 2012, *H+* would be joined by many more big-budget web series with Hollywood names attached. On September 25th, *Cybergeddon*, created by Anthony E. Zuiker (creator of *CSI*) in cooperation with Yahoo! Screen and Symantec, premiered exclusively on Yahoo.com. It's one of the most expensive web series to date with a reported budget of $6 million. And on July 17th, the animated post-apocalyptic science fiction web series Tom Hank's *Electric City* premiered on Yahoo.com, with an estimated budget of $2 million.

2013 proved that big-budget productions were just warming up with a huge year for Netflix premiering *House of Cards*, *Hemlock Grove*, *Orange Is the New Black*, and more original programming. Followed closely by Amazon releasing 12 pilots, including a *Zombieland* series, for viewer feedback on which ones should be expanded into full seasons. Then on April 29, 2013, Yahoo announced they are joining the original online content game with six original shows in development.

The year 2013 is also the year of the return of two long-running soaps formerly on ABC. Soap operas *One Life to Live* and *All My Children* came back to life on Hulu and iTunes via The Online Network on Monday, April 29th. Unfortunately their return wouldn't last long and by September of the same year they are both canceled. Their return was riddled with problems, including a lawsuit with ABC, disputes over wages and benefits with the International Alliance of Theatrical Stage Employees, and the unpopular move of cutting back on episodes per week.

We also saw more web series popping up on traditional television. On July 11th, 2010, the original Season One episodes of *Children's Hospital* began airing on Cartoon Network's Adult Swim. Original Season Two episodes began airing on August 22nd, becoming one of the earliest web series to make the transition to traditional television.

It would be followed by another series on July 19th, 2011, when *Web Therapy* premiered on Showtime. The series would also continue on the web. Another web series that transitions to traditional television, but this time also keeps its web presence instead of fully transitioning to television.

And on October 22nd, 2011, a second "Fred" movie premieres on Nickelodeon, called *Fred 2: Night of the Living Fred*, this time with a rating of 5.7 million viewers. The success of the two "Fred" movies spawns a Fred television series on February 20th, 2012, called *Fred: The Show*.

The Annoying Orange joins in the web series to traditional TV invasion by premiering on cable television as *The High Fructose Adventure of the Annoying Orange*. The series premiered to 2.6 million viewers on June 11, 2012, on the Cartoon Network.

The IAWTV had a very successful awards show on January 12th, 2012. The First Annual IAWTV Awards show was held as part of the annual International Consumer Electronics Show (CES) in Las Vegas, Nevada. The IAWTV broke away from their association with the Streamy Awards to create this new award show which was met with positive reviews. But don't count the Streamy's out, as Tubefilter teamed up with Dick Clark Productions to continue the Streamy Awards. On February 17th, 2013, they hosted the 3rd Annual Streamy Awards at the Hollywood Palladium in Los Angeles, California. With live music guests (including Vanilla Ice) and celebrity guests, the show was considered a big improvement over the 2nd Annual Streamy Awards show. It remains to be seen though if the show will continue.

But don't worry, it isn't all about Hollywood swooping in on web series. On November 26th, 2011, "JourneyQuest" Season Two raised $113,028 on Kickstarter, breaking many crowdfunding records for web series at that point. And those creators, Zombie Orpheus Entertainment (ZOE), would surpass that in 2012 with their movie *Gamers 3* (which will premiere online), by raising over $400,000 on Kickstarter, breaking nearly all records for film and web series (see Chapter 3 for more Kickstarter campaigns). That is, until Freddie Wong's Kickstarter campaign for Season 2 of *Video Game High School* raised a whopping $808,341 on February 12, 2013.

If any more proof was needed that web series have grown into a medium with a substantial audience, that proof arrived in

March of 2014. On March 11th, the President of the United States appeared on a web series. President Obama made an appearance on Zach Galifianakis' Funny or Die web series, *Between Two Ferns*, in an attempt to reach young audiences. And later that month Disney officially announced they were buying YouTube multi-channel network Maker Studios for $500 million. Maker Studios hosts 55,000 channels, with 380 million subscribers and 5.5 billion views per month.

Now Towards the Future

As you can see, while film and television history has developed over many decades, advances in new web television distribution have been moving at lightning speed. The ever evolving web television community has also been growing quickly and changing dramatically almost yearly. And remember, we are still in the middle of the revolution, so the changes will not be slowing down any time soon.

Here are some stats on how many people are watching web television:

- According to a study by the IAB (Interactive Advertising Bureau) and GfK released in May 2013, an estimated 45 million Americans view original, professionally produced online video (OPOV) content every month. That's one in five (19%) persons age 18+ are watching OPOV. Notice I said original online programming. This is content made to be viewed first on the web. That is not including what they call User Generated Content (i.e. funny cat videos or family videos on YouTube) or Online TV which are shows that first air on traditional TV and then air online.

- On May 2013, YouTube claimed at the Digital Content NewFronts that YouTube now currently averages more than one billion monthly uniques, which is about 15% of the world's population.

- In the first quarter of 2013, Netflix reported 29.17 million domestic subscribers, surpassing HBO for the first time.

- Hulu reported in their first quarter of 2013 that they now have more than four million paying subscribers to its Hulu Plus service and the number of subscribers has doubled since last year. Hulu also reported that they streamed more than one billion videos in the first quarter of 2013.

So there are a lot of viewers out there and their numbers are growing quickly each year. But enough with the past; now let's look toward the future.

So, where is this leading us? It seemed in the early days that, with some creativity and good writing, you could stick an improv actor in a ninja outfit, put him in front of a green screen, and make millions ... because *Ask A Ninja* did that very thing in 2007. But as bigger Hollywood names start jumping on board, they are taking the attention away from independent television producers while also not making profit at the levels they are familiar with, leaving everyone frustrated. How the heck do we make this work? Keep reading and I'll show you how to develop a strong strategy for your own series.

Why a Web Series?

One of the first questions you should ask yourself is why you want to work in the web television field. Before I go into that more, I'll share with you what Joel Bryant, actor and producer of *Suck & Moan,* shared with me a few years ago.

"The thing I love about new media and the new media community is everyone is very proactive. It goes back to Felicia Day's acceptance speech at the 1st Streamy's, where she had a bunch of doors slammed in her face and people wouldn't give her this or give her that. So she just went out and created what she wanted to create," said Bryant. "I think that is the beautiful thing about new media. I think it is truly the new independent production. People make indie films now, but it's like — 'Our new film starring Sean Penn and Paul Newman, directed by Clint Eastwood.' That's not an independent film! It's the new Do-It-Yourself entertainment. The technology is there and the outlets are there. It's giving all sorts of people a voice. It's an exciting community to be a part of."

So now let's talk about the advantages of this DIY independent web television medium. I've covered a lot of the advantages already, but let's list them clearly as to why you may want to make your next project for web television.

- NO RULES: The #1 reason is that there are no rules! You have strict format guidelines for traditional television (commercial breaks, 30- or 60-minute time slots, etc.) and still some guidelines or expectations from traditional movie formats. But on the Internet there are no rules. You need to make an entertaining series or film that will hopefully appeal to a niche, but there aren't many rules past that. I'm not kidding when I say this is the new frontier for entertainment. Of course, with that breaking-ground situation comes the hardships of figuring out what works, but with that comes great creative freedom and opportunities.

- Distribution Opportunities: Getting a traditional distributor is a great challenge, much less make a deal that will create real profit. But with the Internet you have a cheap if not free distribution option that can potentially reach anyone around the world.

- Engaging With Your Audience: Since you are already on the web, the ability to interact with your audience is a natural extension of your project. It can be through comments on your YouTube or Blip channel, your Twitter account, Facebook page, or the almost endless other options you have available. You can even use transmedia marketing methods to allow even a greater level of engagements with audiences. There have been some great experiments done on web television over the last few years.

- Serial Storytelling: If you love telling a serial story rather than stand-alone movie type of stories, then this is a fantastic way to develop your series storytelling skills and live that dream of being a television series creator. Actually getting into traditional television is extremely hard, but a web series is a great way to make that series you want to make the way you want to, plus it can give you the experience you need to perhaps break into traditional television someday.

Is It a Web Series or Something Else?

So, you've got a story and you think it would be perfect for a web series. STOP ... before you go too far, you need to see if your story is truly a good fit for a web series.

- Does your story take place with heavy in-depth conversation, using few locations and focusing on an issue or relationship? Then you may have something more fitting for a **play**.

- Got a story that explores the mind of a central character, perhaps with lots of narration? Then your story may work better as a **novel**.

- Perhaps you have one clear thought that you want to express... then you may have a **song** or **poem**.

- You have a story that can be told visually through pictures with dialogue and relies heavily on external events to show rather than tell. But, your characters' story can be told in just a major story arc. Then you may have a **movie**.

- Got a visual story like above, but characters with enough depth and story potential to create many stories that can continue for years? Then you may have a **TV series**.

- You have a visual story like a TV series, but it can be told in a compact format. Episodes can be under 15 minutes and the pacing will keep an audience's attention long enough so that they won't click away on the computer. Then, you may have a **web series**.

What Is Your Goal?

So, why do you want to make this web series? Hopefully it isn't to become rich and famous, because everyone would wish for that ultimately. You need to define what your primary goal is for the web series:

- Exposure: You hope the series will help launch your career.

- Stepping Stone: You want the web series to create enough popularity to help you transform it into a traditional TV show or movie.

- Pocketbook: You simply want to make money.
- The Next "Joss Whedon": You want to build a fanbase to help you make future projects.
- A Message: You want to create a web series that will share an important message or help create change in the world.

Figuring this out early on will help you choose how you format the web series. For example, if you are using it as a stepping stone, then you need to make sure you can quickly transform the series into the eventual format you want it to be, whether that is making sure your season can be combined into TV episodes or a feature-length film, or having scripts ready for the end format structure.

Who Is Your Audience?

So you now know that your rough story will fit the web series format and you've defined your goal for this project. Now you need to figure out who wants to see this story on the little or (if you have a smart TV) big screen. You could roll the dice and hope that this story will appeal to an audience, but if you want real success, based on one of those goals we talked about before, you need to do better than that. You need to find a niche audience that wants a story like this, ideally a niche that truly hungers for this story. Not only will this help you in your marketing plans to reach that audience, but you can make sure this story will appeal to them. This niche or niches will be your core audience.

What's an example? Let's take one of the best known web series out there, the comedy *The Guild*. Felicia Day was an actress who was having trouble finding steady work. Besides a successful stint on *Buffy the Vampire Slayer* and commercial work, she was having a challenge getting productions to accept her for parts. So, after some online gaming bingeing, she struck on an idea. Why doesn't she make her own project she can star in? Web savvy, she decided to make her own series, which she would star in.

But what to make it about? Well, she is an admitted gaming addict, *World of Warcraft* being her poison of choice. Not only would making a web series about gamer addicts playing a game similar to one of her favorites be true to her creative point of view, but it was obvious with the hit of the *Halo* machinima parody *Red vs. Blue* that gamers were already online and would flock to creative content that spoke them. So Day made a web series in 2007, when original content on the web was still in its infancy, and it became a hit. Of course, I'm oversimplifying how she made it a hit; it took excellent writing, acting, and marketing, but she started with a strong base. She recognized a niche that she could make a story. one for which she cared about, too. That is what you need to do also.

Want another example? Let's take a look at a production company of friends fresh out of college. They called themselves Dead Gentlemen and they made a low-budget film called *Gamers* which followed a D&D-type gaming group showing us the real world and their fantasy world, often with comical results. Their little movie gained a small cult following from tabletop gamers starting with the premiere at the large gaming convention Gen Con. That could have been the end there, but they recognized when they hit a niche that was under-served: tabletop gamers who wanted movies or series that would appeal specifically to them. They went on to make a more traditionally funded independently produced film, which had some success on DVD, but it didn't make them much money.

They felt there had to be a better way to make something that would appeal to tabletop gamers, but also gave them creative control and possibly real profits. So they created a production company called Zombie Orpheus Entertainment (ZOE) whose goal was to self-distribute content that would appeal to this small but loyal fanbase. They were inspired by the open gaming license movement in tabletop gaming (by which game publishers made their rule system copyright-free), where unlicensed individuals could now make their own products for game lines. Applying this type of fan-powered/copyright-free concept with distribution via the Internet, they decided to make a comedy web series called JourneyQuest, which would be realized under a Creative Commons license allowing fans to share the episodes legally as long as no profit was sought. This also allowed fans to make subtitles, fan art, and much more.

JourneyQuest became a hit after premiering at Gen Con. Riding its growing popularity from Season 1 and ZOE's concept of the fans being the ones who decide the future of the series, they launched a successful Kickstarter for Season 2 raising over $113,000. They followed that success with another successful Kickstarter for their third Gamers film, which raised over $300,000.

ZOE turned a small cult hit film and expanded it into a successful web series and film series. They did this by recognizing a niche hungering for unique content aimed at them (tabletop gamers) and understanding that the basic Open Gaming License concept applied to film via Creative Commons would be appreciated by this audience and benefit them in crowdfunding, a concept they call "creator distributed, fan supported." Now this sort of Tabletop/Roleplaying Game comedies sub-genre has exploded with similar web series: *Standard Action, Brothers Barbarian, Monday Knights, One Hit Die, Gamer Chick*, and many more. Each have had varying levels of success, but it is obvious that a need for a niche was seen and ZOE successfully filled it and helped inspire others to create similar types of works.

So there you go. Find a niche, ideally one you are already in as a fan. But if you aren't, then you better truly become passionate for it or it will show. Please don't become a pretender and find a niche you know nothing about and try to make something for them. Failure will be almost certain.

The Right Title, The Right Brand

Once you have your concept down for your series, you'll need to come up with a catchy title. It needs to be memorable, to capture the feeling you are going for, and to stand out.

A Warning About Titles

Remember: your title just isn't a title, it is your brand. You need to make sure it isn't confused with something else similar. And ... you may want to think twice about a title that is just one word, unless it is spelled in an unusual way. Why? Because even if you did an extensive Google search and can't find anyone using that title, it doesn't stop them from picking it up later. "But Marx," you say, "they are just clouding up their brand." Possibly true, and most likely a bad move on their part if they are an independent like you. But ... what if they aren't independent?

Let me share with you the cautionary tale of the sci-fi web series *Continuum*. Blake Calhoun created the award-winning web series *Pink*, then went on to do other web series work like Warner Brothers' series *Exposed*. He had some great success and could conceivably be called one of the more successful web series creators in the early years. It also seems he has a habit of using one-word titles. Hey, it worked for him so far, right? So when he created a new sci-fi web series about a woman who wakes up on a spaceship with no memory of her past, Calhoun thought the title *Continuum* would be great. It is, and the series found a following ... but someone else decided that *Continuum* was a cool name too, and suddenly, a Canadian science fiction TV series popped up with the *Continuum* title also.

Now before you cry foul, remember you can't copyright titles, and this TV series has a very different concept: a female police officer from the future accidentally becomes trapped in our present day with a number of escaped prisoners from her time. This is very different from Calhoun's story of a woman with no memory who wakes up on a spaceship seemingly alone except for the ship's artificial intelligence.

So, is this just bad luck? Sort of. The creators of the TV series have admitted publicly that they knew about the web series with the same name which premiered before their show... but *they didn't care*. That's right folks, although there is an almost unwritten law in television to not re-use a series title while that show is on the air with new episodes, traditional television does not apply that rule when considering independent web series.

I'm not trying to paint anyone as the bad guy here. No one broke any laws and I'm sure no malice was intended. But to say a sci-fi series premiering on Canadian television with the same name as that of a web series didn't affect said web series would be a lie. Plus, that TV *Continuum* was a hit show in Canada and soon after got picked up by the SyFy Channel to air in the United States. What was the fallout for Calhoun's show? A confused audience. The web series got countless visitors to their social networking sites who were confused and some were even angry that they searched for the traditional TV show only to find a web series that was very different. Is this the end of the world for Calhoun's show? Of course not. The show won multiple IAWTV Awards and has a great fan following. And you could even argue that they benefited from the attention of the TV show, but it likely was a complication that they would have preferred to avoid. And the chances of Calhoun's show getting picked up for traditional television probably disappeared, unless a title change was done.

Be careful when you pick a title. Stay away from a one word title with traditional spelling, unless you are prepared for a *Continuum* scenario. And also, do your homework and make sure you aren't unintentionally using a title of a currently airing series.

Fan Productions and Adaptations

There is no doubt that fan productions are popular on the Internet and have been for almost as long as the bandwidth could handle streaming video. The idea of fans making their own versions of new stories in an already existing world has been around before the Internet became popular, but the web gave these fans an easy way to distribute and market these projects. The best examples are *Star Trek* fan productions. Besides the long lasting and popular *Star Trek: Phase II,* which I've mentioned before, there are many more examples, including *Star Trek: Hidden Frontier, Star Trek: Renegades, Star Trek Continues,* and many more. Some of them even have guest stars who were actually in the official *Star Trek* series or films.

Each project has had varying life spans and levels of success, but there is no doubt they garnered attention by *Star Trek* fans. Off-shoots of *Star Trek* aren't the only fan productions being made; there are plenty of productions made by fans of *Star Wars, Batman, Doctor Who, Lord of the Rings,* etc. Some of these are films and others are web series, but all of them have a fanbase larger than the typical first season of an original web series or first film by a new director.

If you are a new filmmaker and eager to leave an impression, one possible choice would be making a fan web series or film. You already know there is a niche for it and if you are a fan of the story setting, it wouldn't take much work for you to find fellow fans online and spread the word. If you do a good job, it will create a large enough buzz that you may be able to ride into an original series or film from which you could profit. Oh, that is one important thing to note. You can *not* make a fan production into a profitable business ... well, you could, but be ready to get sued at some point. This type of production means you trade attention for possible profits. If you are early in your career, however, that may be a fair trade to make.

And here is another thing that needs to be mentioned: For the most part, Paramount has been accepting of *Star Trek* fan productions as long as they are credited, but that isn't always the case for other fan productions. If you decide to make a fan production, do some research to see if there are other productions in this story setting. If there are not, it may be because the creators/owners of the product identity are not willing to turn a blind eye to fan productions. There is no legal reason why they have to allow you to make a fan production, profitable or not. So, if you are treading into the new frontier of a fan production setting for a particular series or film, you may want to be careful. Perhaps reach out to them to let them know you are making this production. It is stressful, because they could say no, but is making the production only to be shut down later really any better?

On a related note, this is where you get official permission to adapt or perhaps make a sequel to an existing product identity, typically a novel, graphic novel, or game. However, I haven't seen a lot of these in web television, likely because many independent web series creators want to tell their original stories, are happy to make a fan production, or they don't have the connections to get the rights to adapt an existing work. One recent example I can think of that had a successful Kickstarter ($81,753) is *Morganville: The Series*. This web series is an adaptation of the *New York Times*, *USA Today*, and internationally bestselling *Morganville Vampires* novels. Texas author Rachel Caine had been trying for years to turn her 15-book saga into a movie or TV show, but traditional Hollywood deals all floundered. But then, Felicia Day introduced Texas director/producer Blake Calhoun (*Continuum*) to her and the two teamed-up to adapt her books into a web series. The Kickstarter was a success and it provides a good example of an adaptation option.

Found a niche which you are passionate about, but don't have a story to tell? You might be able to find an already existing story in another medium that would appeal to that niche. But if you go that route, just make sure you truly understand that niche and you are passionate about the story you are adapting.

CHAPTER 2

BUILDING THE PERFECT SERIES

"Figure out exactly what your show is. That helped us a lot moving forward, we were able to explain quickly to people what the show was. And have fun with it." — Dan Williams creator, writer, producer of *Asylum*

Here are a few tips I want to provide you to prevent some common mistakes. Remember, the script is your blueprint. A small flaw there could create a crack in the foundation of the story you are building, which could grow during production and post-production ... leading to the whole story collapsing. So let's go over some nuggets of wisdom I would like to share.

I hope it goes without saying that your script is crucial to the success of your project. Michael Flores, producer of the gritty supernatural western series *Western X*, said it well a couple of years ago when he spoke to me about the importance of the script.

"Make sure you have your script. The reason why I say that is because I see so many people that don't even have a complete script before they start anything. That is your blueprint. You can't build a house without a blueprint and you can't tell a story without a script. Make sure your script is tight. Make sure people read it and give advice on it."

So, with that in mind, let's take a look at my **10 Big Tips for Writing Web Series**:

Tip No. 1. The Protagonist and the Antagonist Are Two Sides to a Winning Coin

All too often scripts have a weak protagonist (aka, hero or main character(s) we follow in the story). Even when they don't, they all too often partner up the protagonist with a weak antagonist. Just to clear things up, they are *both* important. Don't believe me? Read *Dan O'Bannon's Guide to Screenplay Structure* which talks all about the need for a strong antagonist in far more detail than I do here. An antagonist (aka, the villain or obstacle facing the protagonist) can be a person, force of nature, group of beings, or even the protagonist itself.

I would even go so far as to suggest to not think about an antagonist as necessarily one thing, but as whatever the obstacle is in the scene or sequence of scenes the protagonist is in. In each scene or groups of scenes ask yourself, what is getting in the protagonists way? In a movie things are often simpler and the antagonist is easily identified, but in a series of ongoing stories the antagonist can change and shift, and really probably should, to keep things more interesting.

Tip No. 2. About Dialogue: You Are Not Tarantino

With the name of this rule I'm kind of being tongue-in-cheek. Tarantino is well known for long dialogue scenes, but don't fool yourself in thinking you can do the same. The attention span of a web television audience is very small, so you have to work hard to keep them interested. There is nothing like a long talking-head scene to turn off an audience. Every once in a while when you have super talented actors, with unique and interesting ways of speaking, talking about something you've never heard about, in an unusual location ... you just might be able to pull it off. But it is a rare thing and honestly not even Tarantino gets away with it as easily as he used to.

Independently produced web series are on a super low budget, so talking is cheap but don't think you can just eat up screen time with it and not lose your audience. Instead focus on making the dialogue *compact* and *powerful*. A truly tight script has little "fat" and tries to cut out any dialogue that doesn't develop characters, illuminate theme, foreshadow events, or move the plot forward. This doesn't mean characters turn into robots and only say directly what they mean; actually, the reverse. Often they will say one thing and mean another (subtext) or have banter back-and-forth with other characters which will tend to reveal information or move the plot forward.

Even with banter, every word should be chosen wisely either to create humor or drama, while simultaneously accomplishing something to move the story forward. Piece of cake, right? Just try your best and always review your dialogue to see if there is something you can cut or if there is a way to word something differently to get the same result but with less words and ideally even more powerfully.

Tip No. 3. Everything Is Conflict

You know what makes a story interesting? First, interesting characters with a goal who repeatedly run into obstacles creating conflict. You need to make sure the lead characters are not achieving things too easily. There is nothing more boring than that. We have a wish fulfillment to see these characters accomplish things we wish we could, but it needs to be difficult for them to make these things exciting.

So fill every scene or sequence of scenes with conflict. This doesn't mean people have to be trying to non-stop kill each other ... unless it is an action series or horror project. Conflict is just one character wanting something and an antagonist getting in the way. So identify what the character wants or needs in the scene, whether it is external or internal: steal something, beat up someone, convince someone to go on a date, reveal a secret ... or all of that at once ... whew! ... now that would be conflict madness in the extreme. Anyway, you get the idea: Make it conflict-rich, and when our favorite character succeeds (or fails) we will care that much more.

Tip No. 4. Start Strong, End Strong

Have you ever heard of the advice, enter as late as possible and leave as early as possible in the scene? Look at your favorite TV show or web series and see what they do in the beginning of episodes to catch your attention and keep it long enough for you to get hooked enough to not click away until the episode is over. You want to start your episodes off strong like this and then when the episode wraps you need to end with either a cliffhanger or a satisfying end if the episode is a stand-alone arc, or perhaps the season finale.

I've seen too many episodes of web series where they end and I'm startled that the ending is so boring. Leave the audience wanting to see more and give them enough in the episode to feel like things have progressed forward in some way.

Also, use rising tension or escalating tension for sequences of scenes or for episodes. This is where you need to look at the bigger picture; not only look at the acts of each episode, but how each episode plays its part in the overall season. Each episode should feel like a rollercoaster of ... something ... action, romance, betrayal, visual effects ... it depends on the genre.

So, using the rollercoaster example, you want to start off with an exciting jerk of the coaster starting, then have ups and downs that eventually reach a climax at the most scary dip or twist of the whole ride. It isn't just about letting the conflicts or tension go up in a straight line as the minutes go by, but to have ups and downs to give the audience a moment to rest before the next turn in the story. Watch TV shows like *Lost*, *The Following*, *Alias*, etc. Try to map out the levels of conflict throughout the episode and see the patterns emerge. Soap operas are another good example. They aren't for everyone, but imagine the task of trying to keep *daily* one-hour stories interesting without a high budget or fancy visual effects. That takes skill, and the writers must be doing something right over the many decades in which soaps have been popular. I'm not saying go and write a soap opera (unless you want to be like the soap web series *Devanity* for example), but instead use it as a case study on how to write relationship twists and turns (with an occasional evil twin thrown in).

I frequently mention the importance of studying other shows and this applies very much here: Not only study the genre you have chosen in some selected web series, but also in traditional media. Then take it one step further and study other genres. I don't care if you are doing a spaceship comedy with puppets, these characters still can have relationship turns you see in shows like *Friends* or *Big Bang Theory*. The quickest way to turn your stories into stereotypes is to not expose yourself to other genres so that those experiences can enrich the genre you are writing in.

Tip No. 5. Concept Gives Birth to Characters That Decide a Plot, Which Leads Us to Theme

I love this saying, which I created. It is like some magical formula that doesn't make sense until you break it up. Basically, your story concept will help you create the characters of the story, which will help you decide the story plots they have. Those elements combined help you shape an overall theme for the season or series.

I'm going to use a traditional TV show I know well as an example, *Buffy the Vampire Slayer*. Creator Joss Whedon has said in past interviews that the concept started with the image of a traditional horror victim, the blonde young woman who is attacked by a monster, but instead of becoming a victim she kills the monster, playing against stereotype. So, now we have a basic concept, a woman that is counter stereotype and instead of being a victim, she is some kind of monster hunter.

This concept gives birth to characters. The blonde is named Buffy to better play off this counter-stereotype concept: We can call her a vampire slayer. But what about the rest of the cast? Well, horror films often kill off teenagers, so if we make her a teenager then she is in high school and that means she has teenage friends and her parents are still very much in play with her life. So then we start to develop these characters: Willow; the book and computer nerd; Xander, the goofy class clown; Giles, the librarian who will be training Buffy; and Joyce Summers, the mother who doesn't know her daughter is a vampire slayer.

But what will they be doing each episode? Why is this town so packed with bad guys? Hmm ... perhaps there is a Hellmouth that spits out monsters or other strangeness giving Buffy and her friends plenty of threats to deal with each week, giving us a good overall series plot, and from it we can develop all sorts of plots, including relationship plots (teenage romance drama), major bad guys (vampires, werewolves, demons ... pretty much everything but leprechauns, because everyone knows they don't exist), parent drama (Buffy's mom doesn't know the truth), and larger plots (overarching season plots that typically threaten the end of the world). But the most important thing I want to emphasize is that these plots develop more fully as we realize who the major characters are. If Giles wasn't teaching Buffy, then she would approach things differently and make different choices which have different consequences. If Buffy's mom knew after the first episode that her daughter was a slayer or, better yet, if mom was a Watcher, like Giles, that would train Buffy when her powers appear, then you can imagine how plots would have to change. These characters help develop and shape the plots.

Lastly, what began as a rough concept turns into a stronger theme after we develop the characters and the plots ... *Buffy the Vampire Slayer* is about growing up. The monsters and threats act symbolically as life steps that many take upon graduating from high school, going to college, early dating, first time drinking, trying to fit in, responsibility, friendship, the death of a parent, etc. Buffy didn't choose this responsibility and she has to grow into it while growing up; many of us can relate to such a primal theme. This basic concept turned into a seven-year TV series that spawned a spin-off series, comic books, novels, games, etc.

Of course, I don't know the details of how this popular series was created. But you can see as an example how you can create your own series by following these steps. I do believe that this order is important. A common mistake I see is skipping to theme first. That usually leads to a preachy type of story, because the plots and characters are made just to communicate the theme. I would suggest a more organic approach using the above steps. Once you reach that final theme step you will have a story that speaks truth, even if its characters are not real.

Tip No. 6. Characters Are Secretly Chess Pieces

Let's get real for a minute; the characters are made by you and you move them around like chess pieces however you wish. You are playing god and can do whatever you want, telling the story you want. But, like a magician with a trick, your challenge is to make it seem like the characters are living, breathing beings making their own choices and dealing with the consequences.

You can tell quickly when a writer has failed at this. It is when you throw popcorn (or whatever is handy) at the TV screen saying, "... there is no way [insert character name] would do that! It totally goes against what [insert character name] did in episode [insert episode number]!" If you watch much TV you have surely had at least one of those moments. Ideally, something will be revealed that will convince you why it makes sense, but if the writer has failed to do that you will be bugged by the turn and will see the "man behind the curtain" and (in a worst case scenario) might even drop the show if it keeps this up.

I don't like to bring up negative examples, because I know every writer is trying their best, but I feel like I need to give you some kind of example. So let's look at *Star Trek: Voyager,* and I want to first say I am a fan of *Star Trek* and I enjoy the overall series. But, with that said, I had so many "say what?" moments with the characters. Captain Janeway would make one big decision based on some principal she stood for and then on another episode she would do the exact opposite. Then I realized what was happening. The writers *needed* to make characters do certain things to make the plot work the way they wanted, often to work in some kind of theme. Probably they broke rule No. 5 first by trying to force character and a plot into a theme making it feel false. But in addition to that, the characters were making choices not because it made sense based on their desires or history of actions, but because it was needed to further the plot.

The addition of ex-Borg crewmember Seven of Nine to the cast caused more tension between the characters (as might be expected from adding someone to your crew who was once an enemy). But it felt like in many episodes they simply chose a thematic question and had Captain Janeway take one side and Seven of Nine take the other side. This despite past behavior we had seen, making them seem to flip-flop on their beliefs more than a stereotypical politician. It was forced conflict because it was done to make things easier for the writers. It was easier than introducing another character or a new layer to a character to make them a better foil. After awhile it felt forced and I feel it made it hard to take the series seriously in the same way I took the characters from the previous Star Trek series. I don't have any insider information on why certain decisions were made, but I do know that in many of those episodes I felt the "hands" of the writers forcing the characters to move like "chess" pieces. And the story suffered for it. Don't get me wrong, there were many episodes I had fun watching, but I never felt like those characters were as "real" as previous Star Trek incarnations.

So, how do you avoid it? Flesh out your characters and know them well so you can more organically move the story in different directions. This is the phenomenon that writers talk about when they say their characters start to come alive. One key thing though: If you want the characters to clash, you have to make sure they aren't all the same. Give some characters some opposing views. If you have a die-hard paranormal believer like *X-Files'* Mulder, then be sure to have a die-hard skeptic like Scully and let the obvious personality conflicts happen.

Tip No. 7. Be Original ... But Be Careful

> *"Web series is like the new punk rock bands. It's raw and it's real. Don't regurgitate broadcast pop culture."* — John Beck Hofmann, writer/director of *Tyranny*

You want to make a web series that is original and unique to your vision, but you also want to be careful it isn't too different. There are two camps of thought here.

One camp says that people love traditional television and there is no reason to re-invent the wheel. So you should just model your show after a more traditional format and concept. Hey, it works for them, right? You just need to think smaller both in a production budget and in length of episodes. This improves your chances to attract mainstream audiences and maybe even get picked up by a television network.

The other camp says that the Internet opens so many possibilities that you are limiting yourself creatively by trying to duplicate the classic models. Those shows have already been seen and they have more money than you, so you'll never succeed because you are effectively trying to compete against giants that have you beat in every way that money and marketing counts. You need to embrace your independent television creator side and make something different. Experiment with how you tell your story: Add transmedia storytelling, take interactivity with the fans in a way only a web series can, and do crazy things like film episodes that are under a minute, or episodes that jump around time and characters.

One big champion of this more rebellious side is Joe Wilson, creator of *Vampire Mob* and *Play Shorts*. He feels so strongly about this more indie side that he refuses to call a web series by the name *web series*, and feels it should only be called independent television. Here is what he told me once in an interview, with slight censoring.

"How many times in your life are you going to get this much freedom to tell the story you want to tell without anyone f'-ing it up? That is what you can do making a web series, indie TV, whatever you want to call it. You can do whatever you want and say whatever you want."

So, which camp should you side with? First off, you should have been figuring out who your audience is at this point. If the type of stories they like bucks the system, then by all means go crazy. But if your audience consumes more traditionally structured stories, then you may want to tread carefully. I have had a theory for many years—before web series were around and I was mostly reviewing traditional television. I call it Entertainment Taste Evolution. People want to see new visions, but if you take too huge of a jump, they tend to get shocked out of the story and you risk losing them.

For example, if you read books much you'll see some of the most imaginative things ever written. But sometimes it takes time for films or television to reach the creativity of books. Look how much more daring and creative television has become over the last few decades. Did writers just get better? No, because these types of creative stories have been in books for a long time. You can debate whether or not it is simply fear of taking too big a risk in a high-risk market on network television, or because networks reach to the largest audiences and want to appeal to the mainstream audience who have been exposed to such type of writing in books. I feel that we are seeing a slow evolution in television writing getting more and more daring. And it is slow because audiences need to get exposed to these new ideas a step at a time. After all, comic books have been around a long time, but comic book movies took a long time to be accepted by mainstream audiences.

So, after all of that background about my theory, what is my suggestion? There is no reason not to be even more daring in web series than current television; just realize that the more experimental it is, the harder it may be to get your audience. So tread carefully and listen to your core audience to see if they accept your approach. Ultimately, your audience is the key deciding factor.

Tip No. 8. Web Series Is Not Half as Good as Traditional TV

For the love of the web TV gods ... don't approach your web series with the attitude that it doesn't have to be as good as a traditional TV show because it is on the Internet. Yes, it is unlikely you will reach the same production value, but go in with the attitude that you will make it as good or better as your favorite TV show. You will most likely fall short, at least in some eyes, but it is impossible to have success anymore with a half-way good web series.

Gone are the early days where a new web series was fresh and new by default. Where just someone having the guts to create something original and put it online gave them audience karma points. Each year web series are at least doubling in the number of new shows and the quality is growing no matter the budget. Audiences expect more from a web series than they did in 2007 and you need to deliver to the best of your ability. So no more thinking you can get away with a weak script, bad acting, or worse. Go in with all guns blazing and hopefully when the dust settles your show will stand side-by-side with the other web series currently out there.

Tip No. 9. Think Before You Vomit Up Your Script (or) Rewriting Turns the Coal Into a Diamond

I can't stress enough that your scripts are the foundation of everything you build your project on. It is the roadmap that decides everything else. A powerful and well-crafted script can cause true cinematic magic to happen. A weak script will guarantee a mediocre or poor series. There are three types of approaches taken by writers for scripts.

The Architect: One approach is to pre-plan the script as much as possible. Plotting out every step, developing detailed backgrounds on the characters, mapping out character arcs, and practically writing out every major step in advance. This kind of writer takes more time mapping out the story than actually writing the script and will actually breeze through the script quickly because so much pre-planning has been done. Rewriting will be minimal and likely more focused on the smaller pieces of the story, like changes to dialogue.

The Adventurer: Another approach, which seems to be especially popular with prose writers in short stories and novels, is to take a journey with the characters. With just a loose idea and knowledge of the character, the writer starts writing and struggles through the story trying to discover it with the protagonist. This approach will mean you will need to do a lot more rewriting to polish the script, because it will likely not be compact, have pacing issues, and will need a rewrite just for adding foreshadowing, since by this approach the writer doesn't yet know fully where the story is going, so the writer can't leave clues in the first draft at all. Writers who use this approach feel that the first approach is just too restricting and that they lose out in the fun of discovering new things in the script spontaneously.

The Analyst: Finally the last approach, as you likely suspect, is an in-between approach. The writer selects three to five crucial events and comes up with the basic idea of the scenes that take the protagonist to these events. This allows for a fair amount of pre-planning while still leaving plenty of space for discovery while writing the first draft of the script.

And You?: So, which approach should you take? I personally started out as an Analyst that leaned towards Adventurer, but I found with each script that with more planning in advance, I crafted better stories and I still had fun in the planning process; so now I'm a firm Analyst that leans towards Architect. I think you'll find with scripts that most people out there should be careful with the Adventurer choice unless they are prepared for a lot of rewriting or they just happen to be a writer that is wired that way.

You see, writers are often procrastinators and have a hard time filling the blank pages with words. I can say that because I'm the same way. One way of thought is to then just vomit up your script. Get it on the page and then you can clean it up. This would be the Adventurer approach. What I would caution though is that you wouldn't construct a building's foundation with no idea of what kind of building you are creating. You are leaving yourself open to needing extra work to fix mistakes or, worse yet, possibly having to tear it all down and start again.

The problem with just vomiting that script up on the page without pre-planning is that once it is on the page it takes a life of its own. It goes from an idea to something more solid. And that more solid pattern of words is so much harder to change now that they are down. It is like the longer the words are on the page the more solidified they become to you, more sacred. This makes rewriting way harder than you expect. So what you will likely have, unless you are very experienced or just wired this way, will be a script that has major structural flaws. It will likely meander randomly with subplots that may never fully pay off. But alas, you will remember the excitement you felt first writing it; that adventure you experienced will have a stronger emotional punch for you than it will for an unbiased audience.

So I would suggest leaning more towards the Analyst or even give the Architect a try, especially for dramas or mysteries. Think on the script a little before you vomit it up on the page. You won't be sorry.

Finally I want to leave you with the reminder to make rewriting a very important part of your writing process. It never fails that there are many ways to improve on an early draft of a script. Once you finish the first draft, put it away for a few days or weeks. Then pull it out of its hiding place and read it from a fresh perspective. You'll be surprised what problems you will see. Start rewriting, start sharing the drafts with your beta readers, and don't stop rewriting until nobody has a major problem that has not been addressed.

> *"Remember: when people tell you something's wrong or doesn't work for them, they are almost always right. When they tell you exactly what they think is wrong and how to fix it, they are almost always wrong."* — Neil Gagman

Regarding feedback from readers, I always remember this Neil Gagman quote. Remember, don't listen to every piece of advice from readers and remember it is advice from their point of view. You need to stay true to your own filmmaking voice and only make changes based on criticisms that you agree with, after thinking about it with an open mind. You aren't listening for their fixes, you are listening to what parts didn't work for some reason for another human being. It may be something unique to that person or it may be something larger that should be addressed, but without fail the "fix" is usually not right for your creative vision, so you have to find one that works for you. This is one of the most challenging things a web series creator must learn; how to see their own flaws and fix them. You are so close to your creation it is hard to see the flaws, like a mother that thinks her serial killer son is a super nice boy. But take a hard look and fix the problems.

Tip No. 10. Ideally, Make It for the Web First

Many web series out there have different origins. Many of them didn't start out as a web series in mind, some were either made in a different format (short film, feature film, TV pilot) or were written that way before being turned into a web series. Some examples include:

- The 26-minute short film *Planet X* which was cut into 5-minute episodes using the next plot point as a cliffhanger for each episode.

- The teen horror web series *Throwing Stones,* which was loosely based on a feature film script.

- The 30-minute TV pilot *Eric Schaeffer: Life Coach.* When it failed to be picked up, more episodes were filmed and later broken down into 3–5 minute web series episodes by My Damn Channel.

- Marc Clebanoff's *No Clean Break* web series, which took the released feature film *Break* (infamously considered David Carradine's last film) and gave it new life on the Internet, broken into episodes that used footage not included in the film, added a comic-book stylization make-over, included new music, and added a voiceover from the protagonist.

There is nothing wrong with *adapting* another project into a web series. Just like there is nothing wrong with adapting a novel into a feature film or a short story into a TV series. But just as you wouldn't just slap together some bizarre Frankenstein monster to create an adaptation for a film, you wouldn't just take a film and break it into parts to make it a web series. It needs more subtleness than that. You'll get a web series made, but likely the pacing and structure of it will feel off. It will typically fail to engage the same way as a story made for the format.

So when you take that feature film script, that TV pilot, or that film that you want to give a second life, make sure each episode flows well and basically follows all of the rules. Obviously you already shot it in one format, so it will be harder without shooting new footage or taking other steps like *No Clean Break*. It is far easier to turn a web series into a feature film (if it is a serial story) than the reverse.

Another thing I see a lot are web series that were written as film and turned into a web series as a proof of concept. There is nothing wrong with this, but you need to rewrite the script so the story flows better for being broken down into episodes. A complaint I hear often from viewers about different web series is that all together as a film they would play fine, but as individual episodes they just don't work. So don't treat a web series as just some stepping stone, but give it the attention it deserves and make sure the story plays out well for the format.

•   •   •

Marx's Top Indie Picks by Genre

OK, up to this point you've got a nice overview of the short but jam-packed history of web television and you are starting to work out your concept. But now you need to do some homework. Figure out what genre or genres your show fits into and check out web series in that genre. Of course you don't have to stop there; check out other genres too. But at the very least you need to be familiar with what other web series exist in your genre to see what they are doing right or wrong. You can also try to tap into their audience, since it is a safe bet that they might like your show too.

Below are some web series that have had success or are well known in their genres. I only included independent productions, because likely that is the level you will be entering in. I just selected a few for each genre, but there are plenty more that could have made this list. You'll probably hear about many of the others at some point in this book. For the sake of being unbiased, I didn't include any of the shows I have worked on as a producer (*Reality on Demand, Book of Dallas*), but a few that I worked on in some other capacity made the list due to their great popularity (*Aidan 5, Star Trek: Phase II*).

Look at the ones in your genre and study how they started, how they are marketed, what festivals they did well at, how they set up their website, how they use social media, and how they structure their episodes. Don't copy them, but learn what else has been done in this genre. Each of these shows started from humble roots and found a way to succeed. Then once you do that, feel free to keep exploring other web series on these lists to see if you can learn something from them. Even if they aren't in the same genre, they surely have lessons to teach.

Science Fiction

- **Aidan 5**: *Aidan 5* is a science fiction noir story set in a futuristic city dealing with a conspiracy involving cloning. It has a unique, eye-catching living comic book style of visual storytelling. Season 1 is composed of 16 episodes, and this award-winning series is not from a typical US coastal city, but instead is made by an all-volunteer cast and crew in Columbus, Ohio. Starting as a 48-hour film, *Aidan 5* was expanded into a web series and uses a unique method. Except for the actors and props, everything in the environment is added in post production. Green walls are

Scifi-noir series *Aidan 5*, courtesy of Aidan 5 Productions LLC

replaced with black and white illustrations making this web series a living graphic novel. You can learn more about it at: http://www.aidan5.com/

  - Style: Black-and-white, noir tone with writing and lighting, green screen backgrounds, and visual effects. This gives it a unique look compared to other series.

  - Marketing: Although not as active in social media as some other indie web series and despite not being filmmakers on one of the coasts, they have done something right. They prove that no matter where you live you can get attention for your show. They do have excellent professional-looking promotional pictures and artwork.

  - Structure: The episodes break the rule of making short episodes and are longer than many others.

  - Distribution: Season 1 premiered on their YouTube channel and expanded out to other networks.

- Casting: Mostly Ohio talent, but they do work with SAG-AFTRA. Season 2 had Richard Hatch (*Battlestar Galactica*) make an appearance.

● *Continuum*: This independently produced sci-fi series is created by Texas filmmaker Blake Calhoun (*Pink*, *Exposed*) who already had some experience with web series, but this was his first dip into sci-fi. The series about a woman who wakes on a spaceship with no memory has so far two seasons totaling 18 episodes. Episodes are available on Video-On-Demand, the indie TV subscription network JTS.tv, and YouTube via SciFi Riot and its own YouTube channel. http://watchcontinuum.com/

- Style: The series built a starship set adding great art department production value rarely seen on web series and has a cinematic approach to the camera work.

- Structure: It is a serial format where each episode ends on a cliffhanger to urge you to want to check out the next episode as the story slowly reveals its mysteries.

- Distribution: *Continuum* is given a staggered release using multiple and respected distribution platforms.

- Casting: The series uses actors known in the web series community, Melanie Merkosky (*Lonelygirl15*, *Harper's Globe*) and vlogger/actress Taryn O'Neill (*After Judgment*).

● *Mercury Men*: Created by writer/director Christopher Preksta, this retro shot black-and-white sci-fi series about Earthlings fighting men from the planet Mercury was shot in Pittsburgh on a budget under $10,000. There are ten online episodes, each approximately seven minutes long. www.mercurymen.com

- Style: The series has a very retro 1950s pulp sci-fi feel to it and is shot in black-and-white, but the story is actually set in 1975. The visual effects are well-done, especially the Mercury Men who are actually Preksta in costume.

- Distribution: While in post-production it was picked up by the SyFy channel and shown on their website.

41

- Marketing: The series did a great job promoting itself, gathering a fanbase and catching the attention of SyFy.

- **Pioneer One**: One day in New York, Josh Bernhard and Bracey Smith hit upon a series concept that struck a creative cord, so they decided to seek funding from viewers on the Internet to make the series a reality. Their fundraising approach combined with a peer-to-peer release method has been a great success for them. The *Pioneer One* plot is as much *West Wing* as it is *X-Files*. An old Soviet space capsule falls out of the sky and a man is found inside who claims to have been born on Mars to two Soviet cosmonauts in the 1980s. The series deals with the political and social fallout. http://vodo.net/pioneerone

  - Style: Very much *West Wing* meets *X-Files*, with more talking and mysteries than action or heavy visual effects. This makes the production manageable and creates a style that traditional television viewers are used to, while giving it a creative spin.

  - Structure: The series has very long episodes compared to many of the other web series, with episodes that run 30 minutes or more.

  - Distribution: *Pioneer One* uses a very unique approach to distribution. They teamed up with VODO to release the series using peer-to-peer or torrents. When you hear the words peer-to-peer or torrent you probably first think of pirates. (Not the Johnny Depp 'arrr' pirates, but the online variety.) But not all torrents are pirated; some are released by the creators themselves and this is one of the few web series to use this method of distribution. Within two weeks of its release, the pilot was downloaded nearly half a million times.

  - Marketing: They primarily spread the word through word-of-mouth, social media, and major bit torrent sites. They did something right because they were able to raise $30,000 to film episodes 2, 3, and 4.

- **Riese — Kingdom Falling**: This science fiction–fantasy/steampunk web series was filmed independently in Vancouver and released online on November 2, 2009, under the title *Riese: The Series*. Its high production value and actors from popular sci-fi series prompted SyFy to buy the rights and relaunch it under the new name, adding new episodes and narration by Amanda Tapping (*Stargate SG-1, Sanctuary*). http://www.syfy.com/riese/

- Style: It was one of the first live action web series that used the steampunk genre, used animals (a wolf), and had elaborate fight scenes. It also used the Red One camera which at the time was very rare for a web series.

- Structure: Each episode was around 7–11 minutes long and each episode led to the next, often ending in cliffhangers.

- Distribution: After the first few episodes were released online independently, SyFy bought the rights and released it on their digital channel.

- Marketing: Mostly word-of-mouth on sci-fi websites, blogs, podcasts, and building popularity out of the Vancouver area. They did something right to get SyFy's attention and they created a high quality product that gave them confidence to buy the rights.

- Casting: Allison Mack (*Smallville*)

Super Hero

- **Dr. Horrible's Sing-Along Blog**: This three-part musical tragicomedy web series is often noted as an example of one of the most successful web series. It is arguably the first web series to be a mainstream hit, getting press coverage by mainstream press. This is no surprise considering it was created by Joss Whedon who at the time was well known for *Buffy the Vampire Slayer* and *Firefly*. It also starred a number of actors who were either already well known or would be very soon after, including Neil Patrick Harris (*How I Met Your Mother*), Nathan Fillion (*Firefly, Castle*), Felicia Day (*The Guild*), and Simon Helberg (*Big Bang Theory*). On May 3, 2012, Joss Whedon told *Forbes* during an interview that the web series, including all of the different methods for distribution and related products like the soundtrack, made over $3 million. http://drhorrible.com/

- Style: A superhero musical interspersed with vlogger type of confessions made by Dr. Horrible. The style is very unique meshing together the genres of a musical and a superhero story, while using the vlogger style of appearances that are popular online and also used in popular web series like *The Guild*.

- Structure: The series was just three episodes. So more like a limited series than an ongoing series. A sequel has been in the works but with Whedon soon after becoming involved with *The Avengers* movie he has been too busy to follow it up.

- Distribution: It used a unique release method at the time, streaming online for free before becoming available for sale on iTunes (commercial-free downloads at iTunes for $1.99 or $3.99 for all three).

- Marketing: There was a large press push, mostly gaining traction from the names attached. The press was mostly via social media and traditional news.

- Casting: Between Joss Whedon and the other cast members who all have huge fan followings, it isn't hard to see why it drew attention.

- **Super Knocked Up**: This comedy series started with a fun concept with a spin on the normal superhero genre, a superhero (Captain Amazing) and a supervillianes (Darkstar) give in to temptation and sleep together ending with the supervillianes getting pregnant. Oops. Jeff Burns originally imagined the story as a feature film, but after seeing so many stories moving onto the web he turned it into a web series. He had limited film experience doing short films, but that didn't stop him and thank goodness it didn't. Not only did *Super Knocked Up* catch on, being accepted to nearly every festival it was entered, but it won award after award. http://superknockedup.com/

  - Style: The series does an excellent job in branding itself with a catchy musical theme and with a well-crafted (but quick) opening credit sequence. Although the costumes aren't on par with high budget productions, they work with the comedy superhero tone of the series. A good example of how to do a superhero comedy on a tight budget.

Superhero comedy series *Super Knocked Up*, courtesy of Jeff Burns

- Structure: Fits a fairly standard web series format with each episode being around 5–10 minutes and leading into the other as the story unfolds. Burns actually wrote it originally as a feature film, so he adapted it by breaking it up into parts.

- Distribution: The series is released on a wide range of distribution platforms, including YouTube and many more.

- Marketing: Burns has done a fantastic job marketing *Super Knocked Up*, by using the live Google Hangout show *Super Geeked Up* (which also gets released as a podcast) to not only promote his series but to have guests from other web series on the show. It did a fantastic job helping his series be well-known online. He combined that with excellent promo graphics, strong social media presence, a wide range of festival releases, and a fun mini-series called *Super Mashed Up* with crossovers between shows or their creators. You can learn a lot about how to market a web series from this show.

- Casting: The show started with no well-known actors and actually suffered what could have been a crippling setback for Season 2. Natalie Bain, who played Darkstar in Season 1 dropped out of the production, forcing Burns to recast one of the leads. It is a problem that I'm surprised doesn't happen more often in web series where you face issues on bringing back actors with each season while on a limited budget. But Burns bounced back getting Jourdan Gibson who had some recognition from starring in the web series *Cell: The Web Series*. He worked hard to get fans to know Jourdan with her having *Super-Jourdy* vlogs, which then morphed into the *Super Geeked Up* Google Hangout which still lives on, having won its own awards.

- *Heroes of the North:* This Canadian superhero web series follows a group of heroes fighting against a terrorist organization called Medusa. http://www.heroesofthenorth.com/

  - Style: Fantastic costumes that are on par in production quality with any large budget superhero production.

  - Structure: Episodes are 4–11 minutes long. Each season is broken into chapters with different episodes in each chapter.

  - Distribution: Everywhere, the series is on a wide range of online distribution platforms.

  - Marketing: This web series uses transmedia storytelling through live action episodes, comic books, Tech Sheets, character diaries, a novel, photobooks, and more. It is a good example of a web series embracing transmedia.

Horror

- *Asylum:* This creepy procedural dramatic series premiered December 10th, 2010. It takes place in St. Dympna, a hospital for the criminally insane. After an outbreak of violence, an official from the Department of Mental Health is sent to investigate. The web series created by Dan Williams did well, winning awards and nominations. Its biggest achievement was being picked up by BET and later on Hulu. http://Hulu.com

  - Style: The series has an *X-Files* meets *House* feel to it. It is shot very well with a RED camera in a style of cinematography that would compare well to *X-Files*.

- Structure: Episodes are 6–8 minutes long, with 6 episodes in Season 1.

- Distribution: BET picked up this series with *Lenox Avenue* and *Odessa* to air on all of their digital channels. Later the series was picked up by Hulu.

- **Black Box TV – The Series***:* This immensely popular YouTube channel was created by writer and director Tony E. Valenzuela. The channel's flagship series is the horror/sci-fi anthology series *BlackBoxTV Presents*. Valenzuela already had a history with web series and YouTube. In 2008 he made his first scripted web series, called *2009 A True Story*. After that he worked on *Harper's Globe*. But he really wanted to explore the darker side of storytelling which lead him to creating Black Box TV. In 2012, *CSI* creator Anthony Zuiker partnered with Valenzuela on BlackBoxTV series *Silverwood* and *AZP*. www.BlackBoxTV.com

  - Style: Shot primarily on DSLRs, this series combines compact storytelling, eye-catching cinematography, and well-paced music with twists.

  - Structure: Each episode is short and they are stand-alone episodes.

  - Distribution: Black Box TV is a channel on YouTube and a YouTube partner. It grew from a humble start and has grown quickly on YouTube.

  - Marketing: The channel has experimented with Alternate Reality Games and is very interactive to fan feedback and comments. They always have behind-the-scene videos. They have even taking story ideas submitted by viewers and made episodes out of them.

  - Casting: Sometimes the episodes have web celebs who are vloggers or are from other scripted or non-scripted web series.

- **Ragged Isle***:* This Maine web series is created by the husband-and-wife team of Barry Dodd and Karen L. Dodd. This mystery series follows a young journalism school graduate who has just returned to the Maine island of Ragged Isle. She is caught up in

Mystery horror series *Ragged Isle*, courtesy of Barry Dodd

a mystery involving several deaths by drowning, but the victims are nowhere near water. http://www.raggedisle.com/

- Distribution: Released on YouTube, Blip, and some of the other common distribution platforms used.

- Marketing: The creators of *Ragged Isle* love their home state of Maine and enjoy the camaraderie of other creators who also film there. They created a YouTube channel and website called The Entertainment Experiment for Maine web series and artists. A great way to build a community and help support each others' shows.

Other Series

● *Malice* — http://eaglefilms.com/Malice/Malice_Home.htm

Fantasy

● *JourneyQuest*: This fantasy/comedy series from the creators of *The Gamers* films is about a group of dysfunctional adventurers on a quest through the fantasy world of Fartherall. The series has done extremely well and a third season is planned for filming in 2014 or 2015. http://www.journey-quest.com/

- Distribution: JourneyQuest is distributed under a Creative Commons NC-SA-BY license, with the idea in mind to empower fans to share and remix the videos. The approach has been helpful in motivating fan creations and also encouraging fans who volunteer to make foreign language sub-titles.

- Casting: Mostly Seattle actors, but in Season 2 they did have a few celebrity actors like Fran Kranz (*Dollhouse*) and mixed martial artist Bob Sapp.

Other Series:

- *SpellFury* — http://www.spellfury.com/

- *Standard Action:* This fantasy/comedy web series, based in Vancouver, follows the haphazard adventures of Edda the tiny Elf Barbarian, Fernando the Half-Halfling Bard, Wendy the Sorceress, and Martin the Druid. This picked up the Tabletop/RPG fan base niche partially grown from the *Gamers* films. *Standard Action* ultimately joined the Zombie Orpheus Entertainment family of shows.

Fantasy/comedy series *Standard Action*, **courtesy of Critical Success Productions**

Season 1 was entirely self-funded by producer Joanna Gaskell, who also stars as Edda. Gaskell successfully turned to crowdfunding for Season 2 (Indiegogo, $13,115/131% of goal) and Season 3 (Kickstarter, $36,334/302% of goal). This series exemplifies building a fan base, campaigning for funds, designing costumes, and filming on a limited budget. Not able to afford expensive sets, they filmed in Vancouver's beautiful (but occasionally rainy) forests. http://standardaction.zombieorpheus.com/

Drama

- *Anyone But Me:* This drama premiered in 2008. Developed by Tina Cesa Ward and playwright Susan Miller, this award-winning series lasted three seasons. Originally distributed on

Strike.TV, it later broke away on its own. The series follows a sixteen-year-old lesbian whose father's illness forces them to move to a new city. http://www.anyonebutmeseries.com/

- Marketing: The series submits and does well at a large number of festivals. It is also popular with LGBT media due to the storyline.

● *Clutch*: This Canadian production described as an alt-femme fatale series follows a pickpocket who is offered up to the mob when her boyfriend won't pay his debts. With help, she schemes to steal from her would-be oppressor by posing as his dominatrix. This web series is far more gritty than your standard series, with many episodes having nudity and graphic violence. http://clutchtheseries.com/

- Distribution: It first premiered on Vimeo, but it wasn't long before it was on many of the major online distribution options including JTS and YouTube.

● *Squaresville*: This teen comedy follows the misadventures of best friends Esther and Zelda. The series has won many awards and is a good one to study for how to write episodes that can tell complete stories within each episode even though they are very short. http://squaresvilleseries.com/

● *Thurston*: This Wild West drama takes place in a remote mining town and follows the citizens' struggle for survival in the 1880s Kansas Ozarks. The series has great costumes and includes in their cast well-known soap opera actors like Walt Willey (*All My Children*) and Colleen Zenk (*As the World Turns*). http://www.thurston-series.com/

● *The Booth at the End*: "How far would you go to get what you want?" That is the questions this series created by Christopher Kubasik asks in each 23-minute episode. This series launched in 2010 and is currently on Hulu. The series follows characters who visit a mysterious man in the booth at the back of a diner. Each character has heard that this man can grant desires if they perform a task they are asked to do.

Comedy

- *The Guild*: This is Felicia Day's web series that ran for six successful seasons. I already talk about it in other places, so I'll just leave you with the link. http://www.watchtheguild.com/

- *Jeff Lewis 5-Minute Comedy Hour*: This sketch comedy series starring Jeff Lewis, who was best known at the time for starring in *The Guild*, is a very funny show that runs roughly five minutes each episode. http://5minutehour.com/

- *Husbands*: Created by Jane Espenson (*Buffy the Vampire Slayer*, *Once Upon a Time*) and Brad Bell, the show follows a gay actor and a gay baseball player who travel to Las Vegas in celebration of a federal amendment for marriage equality, but they end up drunk, marrying each other. Worried that a public divorce would hurt the gay marriage cause, they decide to stay married even though they've only known each other for six weeks. The series premiered on Blip, YouTube, and Roku. In 2013 the show was picked up by CW Seed. http://husbandstheseries.com/

- *My Gimpy Life*: This series is created by and stars Teal Sherer (who is probably best known as Venom from *The Guild*). The show is loosely based on Sherer's life as a disabled actress trying to make it in Hollywood while wheelchair-bound. http://mygimpylife.com/

Vlogger/Hosted Shows

- *Sexy Nerd Girl*: This vlog of nerd girl Valerie Lapomme is unique, because it is actually fictional (much like *lonelygirl15*, except more lighthearted). http://sexynerdgirl.com

  - Structure: This series follows the structure of a typical vlog with Valerie speaking into camera about pop culture, gaming, daily events in her life, etc. Except she isn't real, she is played by actress Hannah Spear. The vlog acted as a long-term viral marketing campaign to build an audience for the eventual *Versus Valerie* series which was fully cinematic scripted storytelling.

  - Distribution: YouTube and Blip primarily.

- *The Philip DeFranco Show*: PDS is a fast-paced pop culture and news vlog show created by YouTuber Philip DeFranco. DeFranco is one of the most successful news vloggers out there and if vlogging is something you want to do, his show should be on your list of ones to learn from. http://phillyd.tv/

- *The Flog*: Felicia Day's series, on her YouTube channel Geek & Sundry, where each week she explores new experiences like parkour, soapmaking, milking a goat, etc. http://geekandsundry.com/shows/theflog/

- *Kids React*: Created by the Fine brothers, this weekly series on YouTube has children aged 5–14 give their honest and often funny opinions about viral videos, politics, trailers, pop stars, and more.

- *My Drunk Kitchen*: This half-cooking show, half-comedy series was created in 2011 by YouTuber Hannah "Harto" Hart. It is a hit, another good example of a vlog with a unique creative angle. https://www.youtube.com/user/MyHarto

Other Examples

- *lonelygirl15* — https://www.youtube.com/user/lonelygirl15
- *Daily Grace* — https://www.youtube.com/user/dailygrace

Fan Production/Parody

- *Star Trek: Phase II*: This long-running *Star Trek* fan production, formerly called *Star Trek: New Voyages,* was co-created by Elvis impersonator James Cawley. Cawley would play Captain Kirk until 2013 before casting a new actor for the role. It won a *TV Guide* award and has been nominated for a Hugo award. The production was not the first *Star Trek* fan web series, but it was one of the first and it is the longest running with it still filming new episodes.

  - Style: The series tries to capture the look and feel of the original *Star Trek* series. Great effort is made to duplicate props and sets.

  - Structure: The episodes are filmed as one-hour episodes. Because of this only one or two episodes are released in a year at the most.

- Distribution: Since this is a fan production, profits are not allowed, so it is a free, non-ad supported video distributed via YouTube.

- Marketing: There is a huge following on the Internet that has grown over the years. They reach out to small conventions and sometimes work with other *Star Trek* fan productions.

- Casting: Occasionally the series has had famous *Star Trek* or sci-fi actors guest star: Walter Koenig, George Takei, Grace Lee Whitney, Denise Crosby, D.C. Fontana, David Gerrold, Jon Povill, Norman Spinrad, George Clayton Johnson, Majel Barrett Roddenberry, and Eugene Roddenberry, Jr.

Other examples

- *The Skyrim Parodies* – http://www.skyrimparodies.com/
- *Inspector Spacetime* – http://11thinspector.wix.com/theinspector
- *Fallout: Nuka Break* – http://www.vtfilms.com/nukabreak/

Go Forward and Create!

Now that you've heard my writing tips and been told about (and hopefully searched out and watched) a number of web series, you are ready to polish up those scripts and move forward. The next big challenge is how you are going to fund your new masterpiece. We tackle that next, but before we do, check out some suggested reading for further research.

Sample Scripts

If you want to see other samples of scripts in other formats, then check these links below.

Simply Scripts
http://www.simplyscripts.com

The Internet Script Database
http://www.imsdb.com

Javier Grillo-Marxuach's website (includes downloads of his scripts and pitches)
http://okbjgm.squarespace.com/downloads

Suggested Reading

There are so many excellent books on scriptwriting. Only a few touch on web series, but there are plenty that teach the fundamentals of scriptwriting and that also talk extensively about traditional television writing which can be very helpful. Below is a list of some of my favorites.

Byte-Sized Television: Create Your Own TV Series for the Internet
by Ross Brown

Dan O'Bannon's Guide to Screenplay Structure: Inside Tips from the Writer of Alien, Total Recall *and* Return Of The Living Dead
by Dan O'Bannon & Matt Lohr

Save the Cat
by Blake Snyder

Screenplay: The Foundations of Screenwriting
by Syd Field

Story: Substance, Structure, Style and the Principles of Screenwriting
by Robert McKee

The Complete Book of Scriptwriting
by J. Michael Straczynski

The Hidden Tools of Comedy
by Steve Kaplan

The Screenwriter's Bible: A Complete Guide to Writing, Formatting, and Selling Your Script
by David Trottier

The Writers Journey – 3rd edition
by Christopher Vogler

Writing the Science Fiction Film
by Robert Grant

CHAPTER 3

MONEY, PLEASE

You've got your show concept and script done. Most likely your mind is filled with all sorts of possibilities: elaborate camera work (time for a crane shot), awesome locations (hospitals, mansions, etc.), and big name actors that you are sure will want to be in your brilliant show (Brad Pitt... OK... maybe Felicia Day... right). Well, you probably have to be a little realistic first off, then once you make plans for a more low-budget production, you need to figure out how you are going to pay for it. Most web series funding breaks down into: crowdfunding, branding, studio-backed, fundraising/donations, investors, or self-funding (aka, your credit card).

COMMON MISTAKE: Thinking that you can fund the series from only one source.

Most likely, unless your budget is very low, you will need to combine methods to raise funds. It makes things harder, but there is nothing wrong with it. Typically, once you raise some funds and build excitement, the momentum will help you find funds in other areas. Every dime you raise helps make a stronger product, so don't narrow your vision; try different paths to raising the money you need.

The Frugal Approach

First off, before you start seeking funds, ask yourself what ways you can decrease costs.

- Can you use equipment you or your crew already have?
- Can you rent new gear rather than buy?
- Can you barter services or gear in exchange for services and gear?
- Can actors and crew volunteer their time for credits and (hopefully) a high profile project?
- Are there ways to cut costs in locations and props?

The creators of the sci-fi comedy web series *Transolar Galactica* told me they made their first season for less than $150. This is a futuristic science-fiction comedy series that takes place on a spaceship and involves popping onto different worlds. The comedy angle helps audiences forgive that some things don't look 100% believable, but they did some creative things with what they had. It involved creative uses of green screen backgrounds and their ad hoc approach to costumes and props. Some examples include futuristic guns that are actually Nerf guns and a paint-can opener used as a grenade pin. They eventually got to work with a bigger budget. For their second season, after building a fanbase, they did a Kickstarter that raised over $30,000.

Then there is the advice that *Mercury Men* creator Christopher Preksta gave me.

"My number one advice honestly is very simple: just do it. Don't keep thinking about, don't keep worrying about, don't keep fearing it... just do it. I can't tell you how many times I get asked 'how did you raise the money to shoot *Mercury Men*?' *Mercury Men* was made for under $10,000," said Preksta. "I didn't go to anybody or find some secret investors. All I did was... I canceled our cable bill, I stopped buying as many video games, I stopped seeing as many movies for one year. If you stop spending money for movies and video games for just a period of time, then you will have raised enough money to make a movie or video game or novel or whatever is in your heart that you want to make. The question kind of came to me years ago: Do I want to be the kind of person that is watching movies or the kind of person making movies?"

So, before you decide you need a high budget, be frugal and find ways to save money.

What Is Crowdfunding?

Crowdfunding is essentially the process of asking the public for donations for a project. This could be funding for a web series, but could also mean almost anything from starting a business to making a statue of Robocop in Detroit (true story). It may seem like a relatively new concept, but the concept has actually existed for centuries. One example is the subscription business model used in the 17th century to finance the printing of books by offering perks for donors, like a mention on the title page. Another historical example was classical composers, such as Mozart and Beethoven, who sometimes relied on a type of subscription allowing them to advertise for pledges to finance concerts.

The first recorded instance of it using the Internet as a key component to gathering funds is when a British rock band, Marillion, funded their reunion tour by using online donations from fans. This inspired the creation of the first dedicated crowdfunding platform in 2000 called ArtistShare. Of course, the actual word *crowdfunding* hadn't actually been created yet; that would come in 2006, but the concept as used online can be traced that far back. Many more crowdfunding platforms would follow, including the largest so far: Indiegogo (2008) and Kickstarter (2009).

Crowdfunding has been growing in popularity every year. According to a survey by the research firm Massolution, crowdfunding websites raised $2.7 billion in 2012, an 81% increase on the previous year, with more than half of those funds raised through US websites. The data came from 308 active crowdfunding platforms... yes, there are at least that many active platforms, and no, I won't be talking about all of them; just the key ones that work best currently for web series.

There is no doubt that crowdfunding works for independent projects. A number of web series have found funding using this method:

- *The Gamers: Humans & Households/Natural One* ($30,560/436%)
- *Transolar Galactica* Season 2 ($30,885/102%)
- *The Misadventures of AWKWARD Black Girl* ($56,259/187%)
- *Husbands* Season 2 ($60,000/120%)
- *Submissions Only* Season 3 ($60,400/120%)
- *AGENT 88 – The Web Series* ($104,701/118%)
- *JourneyQuest* Season 2 ($113,028/188%)
- *The World of Steam* ($116,431/155%)
- *Fallout: Nuka Break* Season 2 ($130,746/271%)
- *The Lizzie Bennet Diaries* DVD... and more ($462,405/770%)
- *Video Game High School* Season 1 ($273,725/364%) & 2 ($808,341/127%)

And there have been plenty of films that have been able to use crowdfunding also:

- *The Veronica Mars Movie* ($5,702,153/285%)
- *The Gamers: Hands of Fate* ($405,916/126%)
- *Kung Fury* ($630,020/315%)
- *Hotel Noir* ($81,552/163%)

You'll notice that I not only listed how much each crowdfunding campaign raised, but also the percentage showing how much they went over their goal. This is one important factor to look at when researching other projects. Sorry, you have to do a little homework.

COMMON MISTAKE: Not researching how other crowdfunding campaigns worked or failed.

Similar to the point made earlier in this book, a common mistake made by creators is not knowing what has worked before. It is essential for judging what kind of goal amount is realistic for your audience or what kind of rewards you should provide to meet and exceed the goal. All too often when people ask me to consult on crowdfunding campaigns, they have unrealistic goals, very uninteresting rewards, or make common errors in managing the campaign.

I know, it sounds like manna from heaven... a place on the web where people flock to *give you money* for your amazing idea. But crowdfunding is not winning the lottery, it isn't really free money. Yes, someone really did raise $67,436 to erect a statue of RoboCop in Detroit (huh?) and the 2012 Sundance Film Festival featured 17 movies that had Kickstarter funding (10% of the festival lineup). Although there are some huge success stories and they become more common with each year, what may not be clear is that it took a lot of work to raise that money. So forget any ideas about it being easy money, unless you are a celeb with a following which I'm guessing you aren't. This won't be easy. It is literally a full-time job.

Crowdfunding Research Tools

One way to help you research campaigns that may reach similar audiences is to use Kicktraq (http://www.kicktraq.com/). Kicktraq is a site that, besides listing great crowdfunding news articles, actually crunches the numbers of Kickstarter campaigns. It provides you with an easy way to see the overall data and a chart during the life of the campaign showing how many pledges or contributions it had at any one time. I would suggest using it to look up campaigns that are for films or web series in a similar genre as yours to see how they succeeded or failed. Use it to isolate the best and worst, then look deeper at the actual pages to break them apart and learn from them.

Another variation of that is Sidekick (http://sidekick.epfl.ch/) which is a project created by a Swedish PhD math student who collects data to show real-time predictions of the success of Kickstarter campaigns. The data is collected in an easy-to-use spreadsheet: You can use this to find Kickstarters like yours to see how they fare. I've found that its predictions are sometimes very accurate or way off, so use it as just an additional tool but don't put too much weight into it.

To also help you in your research, if you are going to use Kickstarter, you can check out the Kickstarter Best Practices & Lessons Learned Facebook Group (https://www.facebook.com/groups/KickstarterBestPractices). You can't promote your campaign there, but you can ask for advice or share what you learn with others.

Crowdfunding Tips

Crowdfunding can seem daunting, but don't worry. I'm going to go into some great tips and steps to follow. It should give you a strong start and help you make a successful crowdfunding campaign.

We are storytellers. Our weapon of choice is web series or films, but you can make anything into a story and that is what you have to do with your crowdfunding campaign. Make sure that no matter what, you are telling a story to potential backers and fans; telling them who the creator or creators are, what this project means to you, and why it must be made. In any good story you want to move the audience emotionally, so make sure you can do that with your story about why this project must be made and it can only be made with the help of people like them.

Also, be transparent and honest. You are not the NSA, you don't want this to be a top secret project. Tell them why you need this money (even breaking down categories of costs) and make sure they know who you are, your team, and why this project is important to you. Be sure to share links to your website, Twitter account, Facebook page, etc. Crowdfunding backers back people they believe in, so be sure they know who the people are that are making this project.

Last, there is something to be said about phrasing. How you write your story and pitch can be helped or hurt by your phrasing. According to a study, whose findings were announced in January 2014 by Tanushree Mitra and Eric Gilbert of Georgia Tech's School of Interactive Computing, the language you use could be a *huge* deciding factor. They analyzed over 45,000 Kickstarter campaigns: 51.53 per cent were successful. After controlling for factors like categories, an existing video, funding goals, social media and pledge levels, they compiled a dictionary of over 100 phrases that can, in their opinion, foretell success or failure. Their research found that language accounts for 58.56 per cent of the variance for success.

The top phrases they found for successful campaigns indicated confidence, reciprocation, scarcity, and social engagement ("your continued," "we can afford," "also receive two. . .," "given the chance"). Basically, the creator(s) being confident in their campaign helps make others confident. They found that unsuccessful campaigns used language that lacked confidence and had a groveling type of attitude ("hope to get," "even a dollar," "not been able"). So tell a great story and make your phrasing confident.

Become Part of the Community: In other words, back other projects before you start your own. Why? You'll not only better understand the side of those contributing, but you will show a sign of good will. Many crowdfunding sites display projects that you've backed, so it is helpful to show that you aren't in it just to take people's money but also to help others. It's like karma; a few dollars spent now helping others may come back ten-fold to help you. There are so many projects out there that I'll be surprised if you don't find a few that you'll enjoy contributing to.

And that applies to more than just pledging money. Promoting other crowdfunding projects is not only a nice thing to do, but when it comes time for your campaign the chances are good that some of them will remember and return the favor by promoting yours.

Create a Team: A crowdfunding campaign is a lot of work. You can't just start it and walk away with hopes that the money will pour in. It can literally become a full-time job. So don't do it alone. Find other members of your crew or cast that are social media savvy. Have them help you manage the campaign and spread the word.

Spread the Word: You need to make sure everyone knows about your crowdfunding campaign. Start letting people know before it launches and promote heavily while it is live, especially in key parts of the campaign like the start, when reaching certain percentages, and at the end. The start and end of a campaign tend to be the times that the majority of pledges happen and you want to make sure you start strong to set a good pace for the campaign. Use the advice in Chapter 5 on how to promote your campaign online and offline. The only major adjustment is to make sure you add to your media targets those that specialize in crowdfunding and that you schedule in your marketing plan those percentages reached. Reaching high percentages or getting a large amount in a small time are very newsworthy milestones that will help you get the press's attention.

Make It Pretty: Films and web series are a visual medium, so show, don't just tell. There is a phrase used with blog posts, TL;DR. It means "too long; didn't read." So break up your text with pictures. And don't turn it into a mini-book. We've gotten used to scanning when reading on the web, so keep that in mind when writing your description of the project.

Make a Video: If you are reading this book, then it is safe to say that you are considering pitching a *visual* story to be told on the web. Then video is key for this type of web series/film project. If you can't make a simple video to ask for a pitch, how can you expect anyone to believe you can make your vision a reality? It doesn't need to have the same production value as your proposed project, but you should put some real thought behind it and make sure it has solid sound, video, etc. To emphasis this point, a study on Visual.ly looked at 7,196 Kickstarter projects and found that those with a video were 85% more likely to succeed.

Make sure you cover: who you or your team are, your project's *story* (both what it is about and why you want to make it), key rewards (if you have more than five to seven try to focus only on the ones that are most exciting), possible filming schedule/distribution schedule, and a final call-to-action. Any sneak peeks of the production (storyboards, teaser trailer, test footage, props, locations, etc.) are a big help also. You need to make a connection with the funders, so make sure the creators are in the video. Behind-the-camera talent sometimes like to stay there, but you have to put faces on this project. Don't wing it, make a script and stick to it... especially if being in front of the camera is not typical for you.

Oh, and keep it short and sweet. I would suggest trying to keep the video under three minutes and if you decide to use stills, please don't keep them up too long. The typical default of six seconds is far too long. And don't be afraid to make your audience smile, too. Unless it doesn't fit your project at all or you are just not good at comedy, you should add humor to the video. People respond well to it. Humor builds familiarity and is more shareable from a social media angle. I always say that there are two good ways to bond with someone: make them laugh and/or have sex with them. So... unless you are really desperate for the money, I just suggest making them laugh a little.

Don't Forget Updates: You aren't just raising money, you are raising a fanbase for your project. Make sure to keep them in the loop as the campaign progresses and after funding is attained. Updating during the campaign gives you a reason to remind people you are raising money and urge funders to spread the word. Updates after funding keeps funders happy about their decision and makes them feel a part of the project. Happy funders mean they will likely support you on the next season or next project you produce.

You can do updates on various things: fundraising updates, stretch goals, interviews or other press, new images or other content, new awards, and any big announcements. Keep them informed and try to post new things every few days or every day if you can. Don't let it stagnate and remember this is a long-distance run, not a sprint.

Schedule Wisely, Grasshopper: The average number of days that work best for crowdfunding platforms are between 30 days (Kickstarter) and 40 days (Indiegogo). Unless campaigns like yours have successfully broken that rule repeatedly, I would stick to those ranges depending on whether you are using Kickstarter or Indiegogo. You can go a few more days, but please don't do too many more. I know you think that, surely, with more days you'll get more money, but that isn't how it works statistically. It is human psychology; if there is no sense of urgency then we'll wait and typically when we wait, we forget until it is to late. So create a sense of urgency. This is an *event*, darn it!

Also be careful when selecting your ending date and time. You want to start strong on your first day, so start early in the day and aim for a high-traffic weekday. And set your end time for the end of a day.

You also want to give yourself at least two weeks after the campaign before you begin to get your funds. I've seen people schedule projects to start filming right after the campaign is over, only to realize they won't get their money right away, causing all sorts of headaches.

Remember Your Manners... Say Thank You!: Never take for granted that people are giving you money. They are taking a chance on you and could just as easily give that money to someone else. Make sure to show appreciation for the money they give and their support. End with a call-to-action, combined with a big *thank you* for their time and support. You can also give them shout-outs on your Facebook page or on Twitter. The funders will feel that much more a part of the project and it also provides an excuse to keep promoting the campaign without just repeating yourself.

Set A Realistic Funding Goal: All too often filmmakers get so excited by the idea of people funding their project that they forget people aren't made of money and are not willing to drop large amounts on just anything. These filmmakers often overshoot their goal, which if you are using a platform like Kickstarter means your project doesn't get any money. So the question is: How much do you want to raise (realistically)?

Since I'm talking about Kickstarter, let's use them as an example. Currently (of all categories of projects) 74 percent of successful Kickstarter projects raise less than $10,000 and less than 2 percent of Kickstarter crowdfunding campaigns successfully raise $100,000 or more. Although I'm not using web series or films as an example, those numbers aren't far off of what I've seen in general on Kickstarter for those types of projects and those numbers dip more for other non-Kickstarter platforms. So... be realistic. Aim for what you really need and you can always use stretch goals (more on those in a bit) to possibly raise extra funding for that camera upgrade or "sharks with frikin' lasers attached to their heads" flying down from a tornado just to show the *Sharnado* creators who is boss... you know you were thinking it... okay, maybe just me.

Don't forget when you calculate the funding goal you also need to tack on up to 10% for fees to make sure you are covered, and I would suggest adding another 5% for unexpected problems. I've never seen a film or web series that didn't have something unexpected happen requiring pick-up shots, unpredicted automated dialogue replacement (ADR), or other costly post-production work.

One option for a project that just has to have that higher dollar amount is to break it up in pieces. Perhaps have a campaign for funds needed to film, then a separate campaign for post-production (ADR, music, sound design, etc.) and/or distribution (DVDs, VOD, Blu-rays, etc.).

Please don't let me discourage you from trying for a higher goal. A good example of where that worked is Ryan Koo of NoFilmSchool.com who ran one of the highest grossing film campaigns at that point (2011) in Kickstarter's history at $125,000 for his film *Man-child*. He set a *big* goal to challenge himself, but he did it with some math in mind. He calculated the number of people he had to reach based on the idea that 1% of those who saw the campaign would contribute for an average of $50. When the campaign was done, his estimate wasn't far off. With $125,100 raised in pledges from 2,336 backers, the average donation worked out to be $53. But don't just copy this calculation for your campaign—Koo is talented at networking and was able to leverage his fanbase from NoFilmSchool.com—but use it as an example of how you should be building your estimate. So, you can aim high, but do it with some planning in mind and be prepared to make that your full-time job while the campaign is going.

While I'm talking about Ryan Koo, I can use him as an example of what I said earlier about this being a full-time job. In case you didn't believe me, Ryan recorded the time he spent on his campaign. He spent 345 hours running his campaign (five weeks during the active campaign, plus a week of prep), which averages out to about 8 hours a day. See, full-time job.

So, for calculating your budget you use these questions:

❶ *What's the bare minimum you need to complete the project?* Be honest with yourself and try to cover all expenses. Don't forget to add that 5% for unexpected expenses.

❷ *What are the fees?* The fees vary for each platform (platform fee + credit card/PayPal fee), but the general rule that will keep you safe is to estimate that 10% of what you raise will be consumed by fees.

❸ *How many backers will you have per each reward tier or backer level?* This is extremely hard to predict. But look at campaigns similar to yours and base your tiers on something like theirs. Figure out how many people you will need at each level and calculate how much it will cost to fulfill those rewards. Not just the cost of making a DVD or shirt, but also extra expenses like shipping. I'll talk a little more about that soon.

❹ *What is your true budget?* Now you have a better idea of how much you will really need to reach that first budget number. Pretty different, isn't it? Imagine if you just used the number from step 1 and didn't make any adjustments. You would have quickly run out of money and the project would have crashed and burned. I've spoken to enough web series creators to learn that they had underestimated the costs of fulfilling the rewards, so be sure not to make that mistake.

Speed to the Tipping Point: We humans are an odd bunch. We are reluctant to do something first. Ever set down a cake and not cut it, then see it sitting there untouched until finally you cut into it. Then suddenly it is like an alarm bell went off and everyone realized it was cake time. Before you know it, the cake is turned into crumbs as everyone devours it.

Your crowdfunding campaign is like a cake: people will be reluctant to be the first one to contribute, but after they see other people doing it they will join in. The exact tipping point varies a little per platform, but it is usually in that 20–30% sweet spot. And if you reach that tipping point within the first couple of weeks, the chances of the campaign succeeding are 80–90%. So I would recommend you try to make sure your inner circle of the 3 Fs — family, friends, and fans — can help you reach that tipping point within the first few days. That means making sure they know in advance to contribute and you urge them to contribute within the first few days.

Offer Awesome Rewards: Put a lot of thought into your rewards. Make sure you don't break the bank by offering awards that cost you almost as much to provide as the money you take in. Unless this is a campaign just for funding DVDs or other forms of distribution, where you are basically pre-selling a project already filmed, then you have to make sure you have enough money left over to actually accomplish your goal of filming your project. I've seen many crowdfunding campaigns that have went way over budget, because they offered too many rewards or too expensive awards that drained their money, leaving them to find the remaining funds other ways (aka, their credit card). You want to offer rewards that excite, but this isn't a charity: You need to make sure at the end of the day you get the money you need.

With that said, you do want to make sure the rewards have some kind of value for the backers. This value could be physical, creative, sentimental, or exclusivity. The best approach is to put yourself in your backers' shoes and think about what kind of rewards would excite you or tempt you to contribute towards a higher dollar–rewards tier. Look at other projects, ask family and friends, ask others in your projects team; and one of the best ways is to back some projects yourself. You'll get to experience firsthand what your backers will experience.

The rewards tiers can vary, but some common values that, statistically speaking, do well are: $10, $25, $50, $100, $250, $500. The $25 tier is a very popular amount, especially on Kickstarter. Be sure to add in some high dollar–options, but don't forget these lower amounts. Kickstarter recommends that every fundraiser includes a suggested minimum contribution in the $5–20 tier that offers a reward (say, a mug) for the backer, in addition to higher tiers with more elaborate rewards. Projects doing so are 17% more likely to succeed than ones with only higher suggested minimums (e.g., $50 and up). The $1 tip-jar option is popular, but aim higher for your first tier, perhaps $5.

And remember, you are not just raising money, you're also constructing a community of fans through this process. So put in personal touches and make them feel special. These fans will not only help you with this project, but will be the first to support your future seasons or other projects.

Types of rewards:

- Copies of the web series or film: This is a really basic idea; pre-sale of the HD download, DVD, Blu-ray, etc. Since you will need to price them higher than you would typically sell them, make sure they are exclusive or limited editions with either unique covers, numbering, signed versions, etc. Some popular options for services to use to make these include Easy Disc (http://www.easydisc.net) or Amazon's CreateSpace (https://www.createspace.com).

- Other Merchandise: Shirts, mugs, hats, and other merch can be great items for rewards. Funders like them and they provide your project with more advertising. Look for good deals on these items. Do a search for different options. Cafe Press (http://www.cafepress.com) or Discount Mugs (http://www.discountmugs.com) are two popular options. Another option is posters, but be careful because these can be expensive. You can also offer digital downloads or CDs of the music track. These tend to be popular, especially if the composer is well known.

- Creative Collaboration: Backers get to be an extra on set, have a walk-on role with a line, have a picture of themselves in the series, have a character named after them, send a prop to be used in the production, create a word for a fictional language (*JourneyQuest* did this well with their Orcish language), write a short scene or alternate scene, etc. These things tend to be cheap or free. They also make the backer feel truly like they are part of the project.

- An Experience: Visiting the set, getting a phone call from someone in the cast or crew, dinner with the cast, invite to the wrap party, etc. Again, these experiences come with some logistical work, but they are cheap or free and provide your backer with great memories.

- Mementos: Behind-the-scenes access to pictures on set or email updates sent from the location, live streaming events, signed scripts, glossy signed photo of a cast member, postcards, a prop from the set, or other meaningful tokens that fit the story link.

- Digital Mementos: If you want options for mementos that won't have any overhead, you can use digital versions. Example: include signed PDFs of the script, digital desktop or Facebook wallpaper, etc.

- Scratch My Back... : The production could offer a service. For example, a well-known scriptwriter or analyst could offer to consult on a script, a producer could read a script for consideration on a future project, a writer could offer to write a script based on an outline, an editor could offer a fixed number of hours to edit a project, etc. Think outside of the box and see if there is anything you could offer that could help a filmmaker or web series creator. Obviously it has to be seen as worth something, so these work better if you or someone in your crew is well known in a particular area. I haven't seen them very often, but they can be popular.

- Credits in the project (plus on IMDb) are popular and excellent higher tier rewards. They don't really cost you anything and they are popular. You can have levels like "Special Thanks," "Production Assistant," "Associate Producer," "Co-Producer," "Producer," and "Executive Producer."

Don't Forget Stretch Goals: I've mentioned stretch goals before, but what are they? They are goals that are set to encourage continued pledges after the initial fundraising goal is reached. They typically come with new bonus awards. A campaign without stretch goals will almost guarantee that it will nearly grind to a halt in funding after the initial goal is reached. But more money will help you make a better project, going from bare essentials to a higher budget production. So take advantage of the concept of stretch goals and use them. Zombie Orpheus Entertainment had two highly successful Kickstarters for their Season 2 of *JourneyQuest* and *Gamers: Hands of Fate*. These are two good examples of stretch goals. Take a look at them for ideas to springboard off for your campaign.

Kickstarter

You simply can't talk about crowdfunding and not talk about Kickstarter. It was one of the first crowdfunding platforms and currently considered the world's largest. Since its start in 2009 over five million people have funded more than 50,000 creative projects. Like most such platforms, it covers projects far broader than just web series or film. It also has events, music, stage shows, comics, journalism, video games, and food-related projects.

So, how do films and web series fair on Kickstarter? According to figures provided by Kickstarter, 9,516 film projects were launched with $79,305,924 dollars pledged to film projects and at least 100 Kickstarter-funded films were released in theaters, digitally, or on television in 2013. Not bad, but not every project succeeds. Kickstarter doesn't keep detailed stats on the failures, but so far over 18,800 funded film and video projects on Kickstarter have been unsuccessful. One high-profile failure was Melissa Joan Hart's *Darci's Walk of Shame*, which was canceled when it became obvious that it would not reach its $2 million goal. As of late 2013, the success rate in the film and video projects category is approximately 39%.

But let's not stay too long on the negative; let's talk about some of the successes. In early 2013, *Inocente* became the first Kickstarter film to win an Academy Award, winning for best documentary short subject. For the 2014 Sundance Festival, 19 Kickstarter films were selected. They made up about 10% of all the films screening.

Whether you like it or hate it, 2013 was the year that celebrities invaded Kickstarter. The *Veronica Mars* movie had 91,585 people pledge $5.7 million; Zach Braff raised $3.1 million for his film *Wish I Was Here*; and Spike Lee raised over $1.4 million for his project *Da Sweet Blood of Jesus*. These high-profile film projects by celebrities upset more than a few indie filmmakers and web series creators who felt that these celebrities were taking money away from them and that only independents like them should be using the platform. The outcry was loud enough that Kickstarter felt they had to respond. Their research showed that those projects brought thousands of new people to Kickstarter who have, as of late 2013, pledged more than $1 million to 6,000 other projects. Only time will tell if these celebrity Kickstarters will hurt or help independent creators, but at least for now it seems to have helped by giving Kickstarter greater mainstream awareness.

Kickstarter is like all crowdfunding platforms; they take a piece of the pot. First off, Kickstarter campaigns are all-or-nothing. You either reach your goal and make your money or you don't reach your goal and get no money. Kickstarter takes 5% of the funds raised and Amazon charges credit-card processing fees for an additional 3–5%. When planning your budget, you should just assume that 10% of the total raised will not be available due to fees. Kickstarter claims no ownership over the projects and the web page of the project launched on the site is permanently archived, remaining accessible to the public.

If you are going with Kickstarter, think about joining Kicking It Forward (http://kickingitforward.org) which is a concept in which by placing the KickingItForward.org URL on their Kickstarter project page, project creators are agreeing that they will put 5% of their finished product *profits* back into other Kickstarter projects that do the same. It is an interesting creator movement independent of Kickstarter.

Indiegogo

Indiegogo is easily the biggest crowdfunding competitor for Kickstarter. It was founded in 2008 and has a more international reach than Kickstarter, although Kickstarter has made great strides recently in offering its servicing in countries outside of the United States.

Indiegogo allows you to choose between Flex Funding and Fixed Funding. Fixed Funding is the same philosophy as the all-or-nothing approach of Kickstarter; you only get the funds if you reach your goal. Very few pick that option and instead opt for Flex Funding. With that option, creators get to keep donations no matter if they reach their goal. Indiegogo takes 4% if the project makes a goal, no matter what option you choose. If a Flex Funding project doesn't make its goal, Indiegogo takes 9%.

Other crowdfunding options

Let's not beat around the bush; When it comes to web series, there are really only two leaders in the pack currently crowdfunding them: Kickstarter and Indiegogo. Kickstarter leads by far in much larger dollar amounts on projects, but it comes with an all-or-nothing risk.

But assuming you've built connections on a different crowd-funding platform or feel that neither of those are right for you, here are a few alternative choices:

Seed & Spark

http://www.seedandspark.com/

A relative newcomer to crowdfunding platforms, launched in December 2012, it has a unique model of not just allowing film-makers to gain funding but to help them grow their audiences at every stage: pitch, funding, production, and distribution. It has some major differences from other crowdfunding platforms listed in this book:

❶ This platform is made solely for independent filmmaking.

❷ It's a curated platform, which means you have to pitch to them first to be listed on the site. They say this allows them to make sure they don't have more projects at once that could be funded. I'm sure it is also a good way to maintain a certain level of quality of projects and minimize failure scenarios we hear about on larger crowdfunding sites—never finishing the project or not providing promised rewards.

❸ It not only allows people to fund the project, but also uses a sort of wedding registry system to allow backers to donate items or services needed in place of money. An interesting option, especially if you live in a large filmmaking hub like LA or NY.

❹ After your project is done you also have the option to upload it onto their website. People who give money or loan items gain sparks which allow them to watch the finished projects. So, your audience can watch your web series or film by spending sparks or spending $2.99 to watch a feature and $0.99 to watch a short or episodic.

❺ Seed & Spark isn't all-or-nothing, but "most or nothing," so you do have to almost make your budget to get what they call a green light. The magic percentage for them is at least 80% of the goal.

Although most of its projects to date have been films, web series are welcome. Season 3 of the comedy web series *The Louise Log* raised a little over $22,000 on Seed & Spark. The platform makes money by taking a 5% cut from the money you raise (they offer funders an opportunity to add 5% to their order to cover their fee on your behalf) and 20% from video rentals.

RocketHub

http://www.rockethub.com/

Launched in January 2010, this crowdfunding platform allows you to raise money from around the world and has the potential to have the television network A&E as your funder or provide exposure for your campaign. As of the time of this writing, RocketHub charges 4% of funds collected, plus 4% payment processing fees if the project is fully funded. If the project does not reach its goal, then there are 8% plus 4% payment processing fees.

RocketHub also includes additional social concepts beyond funding projects or what it calls fueling projects. There are options to vote for projects and also to earn badges on the site.

Mobcaster

http://www.mobcaster.com/

Launched in 2011 by a former HBO Go executive, this crowdfunding platform is especially made for independent television shows. You create a pitch video (aka pilot) and if you raise the funds then the project not only gets the money, but will go online at the Mobcaster channel where creators share 50/50 in advertising revenue. Mobcaster charges 5% of funds collected, plus 3% for PayPal charges. If a Mobcaster-funded show is picked up by another distribution outlet, Mobcaster holds 15% participation in the show, per their Producer's Agreement.

Activity on the platform has been slow since the end of 2013, but the platform has raised over $70,000 for two projects and with it being made for independent televisions series it would seem to be a perfect platform. But I'm keeping this in the optional section of platforms because they are still very new and data on how these projects pan out after funding is reached just isn't there yet for me to feel comfortable saying much more on it.

VODO

http://vodo.net/

Vodo is part media distributor and part crowdfunding platform. It releases films under a Creative Commons license using the BitTorrent protocol (peer-to-peer network). So you not only can use it to raise funds, but then can distribute your web series or film via BitTorrent. BitTorrent is often used a little less legally to pirate movies and TV shows, but in this case Vodo is using it to legally allow filmmakers a way to raise funds and distribute their production to a large audience. To date, the highest a project has raised is $100,000. In addition to funding and distributing through Vodo, selected works are promoted on third-party sites and services such as uTorrent, The Pirate Bay, Mininova, and OneDDL.

The biggest web series success using this model is the sci-fi series *Pioneer One*. They were able to raise $30,000 to film episodes 2, 3, and 4. It has also had success with indie projects like the feature film *Zenith* and documentary *The Yes Men Fix the World*. The *Yes Men Fix the World* turned to them when they were sued by the United States Chamber of Commerce: Don't worry, in the end it worked out for them.

GoFundMe

http://gofundme.com

Founded in May, 2010, this crowdfunding platform was created to allow people to raise money for a wide range of events, from celebrations to challenging conditions like illnesses. I have not seen many web series use this platform, but there are a few that successfully raised a few hundred to a couple thousand dollars. GoFundMe deducts a 5% transaction fee from each donation a user receives and, unlike the other platforms I talk about here, they don't require incentives for donations, but the user can offer them if wanted.

Pirate Myfilm

http://piratemyfilm.com/

With a similar angle as Vodo, the Pirate Myfilm site does legal peer-to-peer pirating of creative commons licensed/crowdfunded media projects. It has a pretty elaborate system that I won't detail here, but it involves $5 shares and yellow/green lights. Just go to their website for more information.

With just a couple of hundred projects and most of their projects making low dollar amounts, I'm not sure how useful it will be. With no firsthand experience I don't have much more to say about this one, except do your research to make sure it is right for you before signing on.

Sokap

http://www.sokap.com/ (CAN)

Vancouver-based crowdfunding platform Sokap (which stands for social capital) was originally intended to aid in the distribution of films, but found an opportunity to expand to other types of business. Its goal is to be "… a crowdfunding and distribution platform that allows marketers and funders to connect with project owners."

It integrates marketing and distribution in a way not seen in most other crowdfunding campaigns. It allows you to buy "towns," which can provide you a commission on sales. You also can use the promote button which pays you a referral bonus for every direct referral you bring to the site. There is a bit of a learning curve, but it is an interesting mix of funding, distribution, and marketing. It really didn't pick up steam until 2012 and there really aren't enough projects to get a good grip on how useful this could be, but it is another option you could look into for your project.

ThrillPledge

http://www.thrillpledge.com
Launched on October 2012, this platform focuses on sports and entertainment. One unique element is the site allows project creators to add sponsors to their projects. They have offices in New Zealand, the UK, and the United States. Currently there are no web series funded by them and few projects funded, but in theory a site you might consider for funding a web series, especially if you live in New Zealand.

Sponsume

http://www.sponsume.com/ (UK)
Launched in 2010, this crowdfunding platform is based in London and is most popular in the UK and Australia. It focuses on funding projects like films, web series, documentaries, music, theater, photography, etc. Project owners choose a deadline, target funding goals and create non-monetary rewards. Sponsume claims no ownership over the projects.

Some unique features include allowing users to raise funds in various currencies (presently over 20), translate your campaign in multiple languages (French, German, Dutch, Spanish and Catalan), and reduce transaction fees for charities and non-profit organizations.

Similar to Indiegogo's Flexible Funding option, project owners are able to keep collected funds even if the funding target is not reached by the deadline. The site charges a 4% fee for successful campaigns and 9% for campaigns that fail to reach their funding target. Sponsume has funded over 1,300 projects and the range of their funding for films/web series seems to average around $1,000 to $10,000.

Patreon

http://www.patreon.com

This relatively new crowdfunding platform is based in San Francisco and was founded in May 2013. Patreon was created to enable fans to support and engage with artists and creators: musicians, web series creators, vloggers, web comic creators, writers, bloggers, gamer designers, filmmakers, podcasters, animators, artists, and photographers. It may not target filmmaking as specifically as Seed & Spark, but it comes closer than many other platforms. The idea of Patreon is to bring back the notion of patronage by making backers patrons of their favorite creators. This works best with creators that release content on a regular basis, so instead of feature films, this works better for web series and vlogger-type projects.

Instead of one contribution, you can subscribe to pay so much for every installment or monthly. For example, a patron could subscribe to pay $5 for every video and you can set a limit to prevent an unexpected number of videos to take more money than expected. Milestones are total dollar amounts that, once reached, will unlock content. For example, reaching a certain dollar amount will unlock monthly videos and reaching the next milestone will unlock monthly episodes that are twice as long or perhaps two new videos each month. Creators can also offer additional content based on how much you pay per installment or time period. Some perks are offered, like a monthly Google Hangout with the creator.

Creators can post new content either directly through Patreon or provide links from another distribution platform like YouTube. They can also offer new content as either locked except for patrons or free for everyone.

Patreon only charges you after you make money through pledges on your creator page. Patreon processes approximately 3% for credit-card processing fees and 5% for Patreon to cover operating costs. You can avoid card-processing fees for pledges made with Patreon credit.

This crowdfunding platform is still so new so it is hard to provide web series examples, although I suspect it could become very popular. If you are making a web series that can make regular videos at least once a month, then you may want to investigate this platform.

Building Your Own Crowdfunding Platform

If you have a large existing fanbase, then it may be worth the effort to build your own crowdfunding platform. That is what Zombie Orpheus Entertainment did. Despite huge success on Kickstarter, they decided to leverage their fanbase to set up a subscription service, similar to Patreon in the general concept.

So, if you believe you have a strong enough fanbase, how can you cut out the middleman in crowdfunding? You have two options: Open Source Crowdfunding frameworks or use non-open source software. Below are some options for both:

Open Source Crowdfunding Software

- Selftstarter (http://selfstarter.us/)
- Catarse (https://github.com/danielweinmann/catarse)
- GoTeo (https://github.com/Goteo/Goteo)
- GitTip (https://github.com/gittip/www.gittip.com)
- Crowdfunding (http://itprism.com/free-joomla-extensions/ ecommerce-gamification/crowdfunding-collective-raising -capital)
- Freedom Sponsors (https://github.com/freedomsponsors/ www.freedomsponsors.org)
- Thrinacia (https://www.thrinacia.com/)
- Spot-Us (https://github.com/spot-us/spot-us)
- Akvo (https://github.com/akvo)

Non-Open Source Software

- Crowdfunder (http://www.crowdfunder.co.uk/)
- Ignition Deck – WordPress plug-in (http://ignitiondeck.com/id/)
- Launcht (http://www.launcht.com/)
- Mimoona (http://www.mimoona.com/)
- Invested.in (http://invested.in/)
- Crowdcube (http://www.crowdcube.com/)

There are also plenty of other fairly easy-to-use crowdfunding WordPress themes that are free or relatively cheap. Some examples you can search for are Fundify, Campaignify, Theme 500 and 500 Maximus (for Ignition Deck), Franklin, CrowdPress, FundingPress, Mission, Gig, and many more.

There you go; if you have the software skills, or basic WordPress skills, you can build your own crowdfunding platform, but I stress again I would not suggest this unless you have a large enough fan-base to fund your projects.

Fan Production + Crowdfunding = Caution

There have been fan productions that have been using crowdfunding platforms. If you are making such a project, then you may consider this funding option, but keep in mind you don't own the rights and there could be a downside to publicly asking for money. Although many *Star Trek* fan productions have not had any issues, that isn't necessary the same for all fan productions out there.

Batgirl: Spoiled was building a fanbase and decided to start an Indiegogo campaign in 2013 to help them fund more episodes, but sadly on November 14th they received a take-down notice from Warner Brothers and were forced to end their campaign and return the funds to backers. So if you are a fan production, be aware that this funding option comes with risks.

So, Which Platform?

Now you've just read the breakdowns and advice. You are probably wondering which is right for you. I would say right now, excluding creating your own platform, which would require a large fanbase, then your best bets currently would appear in this sequence:

1. Kickstarter
2. Indiegogo
3. RocketHub
4. Seed & Spark
5. Patreon

It's a no brainer that the highest money-raising crowdfunding campaigns for web series have primarily been on Kickstarter. But it comes with the risks as mentioned previously and is only usable by citizens of a few countries. So, next up would be Indiegogo. Many web series have raised their funds using Indiegogo, especially Canadian web series who can't use Kickstarter. After that it gets trickier. RocketHub has many possibilities and has ties with A&E. I also feel like the younger Seed & Spark and Patreon could become great platforms for web series.

Let's take a look at some of the top fundraising web series out of these top five platforms. It will give you an idea of how much can possibly be made. I do want to stress that some of these are easier to search for data than others, but I did my best to find the top ones.

Kickstarter	Indiegogo	RocketHub	Seed & Spark	Patreon
The Lizzie Bennet Diaries DVD... and More! $462,405/771%	*Hello Harto!* $223,007 US/446%	*Extra Credits* $103,814/693%	*Zompire Vixens From Pluto!* $25,112/81%	*Jordan Owen 42* 2 Patrons/$11 per video
Video Game High School $273,725/364%	*Star Trek: Renegades* $132,555/663%	*Swing Away* $27,945/14%	*The Louise Log – Season 3* $22,065/84%	
LRR's Last Season of Sketches $186,459/138%	*Channel Awesome's New Shows and More!* $89,757/180%	*In Plain View Pilot* $15,858/32%	*Docket 32357* $12,055/96%	
Whatever this is. $171,446/103%	*Laughing Pizza TV for the whole family* $66,921/103%	*Opera Cheats* $6,793/114%	*The Dreamers* $9,948/88%	
Tropes vs. Women in Video Games $158,922/2,648%	*The N&N Files* $65,050/130%	*Eighty-Sixed* $5,000/100%	*Dibs – Season 2* $6,590/101%	

Kickstarter	Indiegogo	RocketHub	Seed & Spark	Patreon
Jeff Cannata's New Show! $151,590/757%	*Captain Canuck – The Animated Web Series* $51,958 CA/104%	*Dog Bites* $4,610/10%	*Ghost Light* $4,971/86%	
Hunting Season: Season 2 $151,406/100%	*The Game Chasers Season 1 DVD* $44,167/1,472%	*Friends or Just Roomies?* $3,550/142%	*Stoner Apocalypse: The Series* $2,740/99%	
A Show with Ze Frank $146,752/293%	*Stellar Gardens* $35,321/24%	*The Girls Guide* $1,255/126%		
A Total Disruption $144,449/150%	*Shelf Life – Season 4* $34,579/115%	*The Pirate Stanley Show* $1,030/21%		
Storytellers: The Series $140,949/140%	*Project Possum* $34,400/344%	*Life After Lisa* $760/22%		

So, what do we learn from this glance?

First off, we see what are the high end of goals we could expect to raise for a web series. Unless you are a well-known individual you would be playing bad odds to try and make a web series with a funding goal higher than these. Films clock in a little higher, but if your primary target is web distribution then these are good "reality check" numbers to look at. Plus many of these on Kickstarter and Indiegogo are second or later seasons, DVDs of an existing series, or have someone well known connected. So, keep in mind these projects already have a significant fanbase to tap into.

Second, we see how web series are still largely unexplored on the newer platforms. At the time of this writing I could only find one example on Patreon, but their search function was horrible for trying to isolate to web series and attempts for help from them were unsuccessful. For Seed & Spark I noticed that the platforms lean heavily towards New York–area productions. Not to say you can't help them expand that, but their "wedding list" option may not be very useful for you if you are the first to use them in your city.

So, what is my verdict after all these investigations?

❶ If you have a high dollar goal, Kickstarter is your best option.

❷ If this is a later phase of the production, like creation of DVDs or in some other way where reaching your full goal is not 100%

necessary and the amount isn't too high, then Indiegogo may be an excellent option.

❸ If you live in the New York–area and have made some connections, then Seed & Spark could be an excellent choice over the others.

❹ If you have a project that can make at least one video a month *and* you have some kind of fanbase to start off with, even a small one, then Patreon may be worth a try. I think this subscription model could really catch on for certain types of projects. But it is still too early to know if Patreon or some other crowdfunding platform that swoops in will be the one to dominate this model.

❺ If you already have connections to one of these crowdfunding platforms, then you may want to stick with that one unless that platform can't reach the minimum funding goal for your project.

❻ Nothing stays the same and with the JOBS act opening new possibilities, there could be new opportunities and some of these platforms may make good use of equity crowdfunding. RocketHub has been very supportive of it and will likely try to be a major player in this new model in America.

What If You Fail?

"Improvise, Adapt, Overcome"
— Unofficial Marine Corps mantra

I probably should mention the elephant in the room: What if your crowdfunding campaign fails? We are trying to be positive and hopefully you will succeed in raising your funds, but failure is possible. So what do you do if this scenario happens?

First, ask yourself why did it fail. If it is because there just isn't interest, then maybe you learned something important although perhaps painful; not very many people like your idea. If this is the case, then perhaps hitting the drawing board and either re-imagining the concept or just coming up with something new might be the best choice for you.

If you feel you failed because you made mistakes in pitching, marketing, having too big of a funding goal, or didn't have a big enough social media following, then you can take some time and re-plan, then perhaps jump to a different crowdfunding platform and try again. I've seen this work successfully for creators who have jumped from Indiegogo to Kickstarter or vice versa.

A crowdfunding failure can happen to anyone. Just ask *Vampire Mob* creator Joe Wilson. After a successful Season 1 he tried Kickstarter to raise $10,000 for Season 2, with people in the cast like Emmy-winner Marcia Wallace (*The Simpsons*) and Tony-winner Rae Allen (*The Sopranos*). On October 30, 2010, the campaign had 140 people who pledged $6,212 which did not reach the goal... ouch! But he didn't give up; right away he started up a simple website and people began donating for the same rewards that were on Kickstarter. Wilson printed T-shirts and he had several eBay auctions for signed scripts and other items. Through this method over six months (and with some setbacks), he raised that $10,000 independently, and so was able to film Season 2 which had an 80-page script with 21 actors.

Last, you could use the fanbase and excitement you made from the campaign and go the independent route like Wilson. It won't be easy, but if you believe in your project, then this might be a good option for you also.

Conclusion on Crowdfunding

Whew, that was a lot of information on crowdfunding, but I think you will find that, for most web series creators who may be early in their careers, crowdfunding is the No. 1 choice and sometimes the only choice. That doesn't make it easy though, far from it.

Now let's take a look at some more funding options.

Equity Crowdfunding

Equity crowdfunding or crowdinvesting combines the basic idea of donation crowdfunding with more traditional investing. It has been illegal in the United States, that is until President Barack Obama signed, on April 5, 2012, the Jumpstart our Business

Startups, or JOBS to legalize equity crowdfunding. This will allow normal everyday people, who don't have traditional accredited investor profiles, to use licensed crowdfunding portals online to invest up to $2,000. I won't go into too much detail about it because at the time of this writing things are still very much in flux. Needless to say there will be a growing number of equity crowdfunding platforms available and likely popular ones like Kickstarter or RocketHub will explore the option, which should open another excellent funding route for filmmakers.

Investors

All filmmakers dream of a rich knight (male or female... whatever works for you) that rides in on a white horse and whisks us away to a forest of trees made of money so we can make our dream web series or film... OK, maybe not exactly like that. But we all hope that an independent investor will take notice of our project and help fund it. There isn't a real filmmaking investor club per say, but they do exist. There are private investors who want to break into the film industry, want to support the arts, or may feel a particular connection to your concept.

So how do you find them? Well, your first option, which probably sounds lame, is... do you know any rich people? Your family or friends might be willing to invest a little money in your project. You could do the old school investing method of contacting doctors or dentists, asking if any of them want to invest. Sometimes this is what you have to do for your first project. Just keep in mind if you ask people to invest in you with their money (even if it is mom and dad), you have a responsibility to do everything you can to make the project a success. If you take it for granted it is a sure way to guarantee you'll never get money from them again, which will kill your career's momentum and you may never recover from that.

Okay, so barring that first option, what do you do next? There are a number of websites and social media groups that have what are called angel investors. These investors sometimes help filmmakers, especially if they are working on a project that has special meaning to them. You can search websites for angel investors, you can find groups on LinkedIn, and there are also groups on Facebook. Do enough searching online and you'll find angel investors. Just be sure you have your investor prospectus ready (more on that soon).

I'll leave you with one potential website you can look into. It is called Slated (http://Slated.com) and is an online marketplace for film financing and deal making. This angel investors group is a platform focused on films and made up of prominent angel investors in the entertainment and finance communities. It provides a way for qualified filmmakers and organizations to discover projects that are seen as viable to engage audiences. There are over 3,000 global members including 400 investors, primarily from North America. Members include filmmakers and actors from films like *Pulp Fiction, Good Will Hunting, Iron Man, An Inconvenient Truth*, and *The Descendants*. To date over 175 film projects have been featured on the curated site.

The only things Slated does is offer introductions; after contact is made any deals are made away from the site. At least six films have found funding from the site. I don't know if any web series have found funding by this method. It may not be a useful site for you if you are early in your career, but at the very least it is something to work towards and gives you an idea of angel investor sites that are out there.

Once you find investors you will likely (unless it is mom and dad) need to make an investment prospectus to help them understand the project and why they should invest in it. It is time to do what you do best: Tell a story. OK, maybe it is a little different, but it doesn't have to be. You and your crew are the characters for this underdog story of these filmmakers wanting to bring to life a story that they feel the world needs to see and (this is important) why they know it will succeed and make money for anyone who joins them for this adventure.

You need to know everything it is possible to know about:

- The Project: What is the project? Why they should be excited for it and who is the rabid niche that wants it. What are projects that have succeeded like yours and how will yours stand out from the competition?

- The Story: Who are the characters and what is the overall series about? Be colorful and get them to feel the tone of the show that will entertain the audience.

- The Team: Who are you and the team that will make this story come to life? Why do they have the skills needed to bring forth this masterpiece? You may want to include resumes of key crew and you could include a short demo reel to show off the skills of the team.

- The Distribution: How will you get this story out to the audience and how will it make money? Despite our best wishes, investing in a film is a high-risk investment. So you really need to have done your research and show money can be made.

- The Production: Do you have pictures of locations? Tell them about the equipment you need and what you will do with it. What is the budget? Show the breakdown on expenses. This is key to make sure you have the money you will need and also that you prove you need the money and will be asking for more than you need. You can show the investors that you are competent with finances.

- The Marketing: How are you going to spread the word about this new series? You've got to prove you have the pulse of the audience that will want this series and know how to reach them.

If they bite, then you'll need to negotiate the money they will provide. Depending on how expensive your show is, you may need more than one investor to share the expense and risk. Or you may need to look at other funding options to fill the gap. Either way, you'll need to draft an investor agreement which you should have an entertainment lawyer look at first. And if you haven't already, you'll need to set up the production company and at the very least set up a limited liability company (LLC). The LLC option is the cheapest and easiest to do. If you don't have a good lawyer contact you can set it up using an online legal documentation service like LegalZoom (http://www.legalzoom.com).

You'll notice that an investor agreement seems like a more formal document version of your crowdfunding pitching and that is probably a good way to think of it. Except there are no rewards, just the promise of profit. And don't forget it is about profit. No matter how much money they have, they don't want to lose and would like to feel confident they can make some sort of profit off this venture.

Branded Web Series

Working with a sponsor can be as minor as a little product placement to as in-depth as building a whole series concept around the brand of the sponsor. Unless the brand has approached you, because you are an established production company, then you'll need to approach them. You'll need to pitch to a development executive with a brief and powerful pitch. This is where that investor prospectus comes in handy, plus a one-sheet that pitches the series on (you guessed it) one page. One thing many branded series have in common is a "name" actor. So you may want to get someone attached if possible before pitching. Your goal is to prove that your series will entertain the audience in which the sponsor is interested, while promoting the brand message and also generating a profit.

Web series with brands backing them have had mixed reviews. Sometimes these experiments do not fare well, but some have succeeded greatly. Often the most successful ones are subtle with the brand tie-in. There have been many examples of these with many different spins on the branded series concept:

- *Easy to Assemble* (IKEA): Created by and starring Illeana Douglas, this web series premiered in 2008 and is sponsored by furniture store IKEA. Douglas played a fictional version of herself trying to quit acting and work at the IKEA. The series ran for four seasons and had several noteworthy guest stars, including Jeff Goldblum, Keanu Reeves, Tom Arnold, and many more. *Easy to Assemble* was nominated for seven Streamy awards, winning two.

It also picked up a nomination for Best Individual Performance for Douglas at the 14th Annual Webby Awards, and won two Webby's for its spin-off series *Sparhusen*. Those are just a few of the award nominations and wins. *Easy to Assemble* is often mentioned as one of the most successful branded series to date and reportedly has had over 11 million views.

- *Leap Year* (Hiscox): UK Insurance provider Hiscox decided to sponsor a web series simultaneously with a US expansion. Premiering in 2011, *Leap Year* is a comedy that follows five recently fired co-workers who turn entrepreneurs and compete for start up capital from a mystery investor. Hiscox has said that the series helped them build awareness of their company in the US, going from 0 to 10% in less than a year and growing their social media following to over 40,000 followers.

- *The Temp Life* (Spherion): A veteran of branded web series, *The Temp Life* premiered in 2006 and is considered the first and currently longest-running brand-sponsored original web series. Spherion Staffing Services is the brand behind this award winning comedy about life inside a NY temp agency. The show is distributed across the web via My Damn Channel, Effinfunny.com, YouTube, iTunes, an iPhone application, on Sprint mobile TV and Verizon VCast via Fun Little Movies, on Roku, Boxee via Blip.tv and on-demand in 1.5 million U.S. hotel rooms via the Best of Web TV network, reportedly garnering tens of millions of collective views.

- *Dating Rules from My Future Self* (Schick's Quattro and Ford Escape): Alloy Digital and Hulu joined forces with the creators of *Gossip Girl* for *Dating Rules from My Future Self*, which follows a single twenty-something Chloe Cunningham (Shiri Appleby) who receives text messages giving her romantic advice from herself ten years in the future. The series features both Schick's Quattro for Women shaving line and the 2013 Ford Escape. This series takes more of a traditional approach to branding by using product placement. The online series premiered in

January 2012 and reportedly garnered 14 million views on Hulu, YouTube and Alloy's video properties.

- *Always Open* (Denny's): Hoping to reach a younger age demographic (18-34) Denny's enlisted comedian Dave Koechner (*SNL, Anchorman*) to star in *Always Open,* where he chats unscripted with well-known stars while eating Denny's specialty dishes in a Denny's booth. The videos are released on CollegeHumor.com and on Denny's Facebook page, and push the message that Denny's is "Always Open" no matter the hour or your age. Denny's claims it has worked, seeing its impression score rise from 6.2 to 25.4 among 18-34 year olds, surpassing the 50+ demographic that once dominated.

- *The Return of D Rose* (Adidas Basketball): With a more reality TV or documentary spin, Adidas Basketball sponsored *The Return of D Rose* chronicling a behind-the-scenes view of Derrick Rose working to return to the Chicago Bulls after a torn ACL. It wasn't until episode four that Adidas introduced D Rose's new line of basketball shoes. The web series also did great social media with Twitter by using the hashtag #TheReturn to get fans more actively involved in the series.

- *Falling for You* (Target): This web series from Target follows Kristen Bell (*Veronica Mars*) and her coworkers as they plan an event at Target. Everything they look at was available for purchase right from the video and used a Pinterest-like element to advance engagement with the audience.

Grants

Depending on what country you live in or the type of project you are working on, you may be eligible for government or private institution grants to help pay for your project. But these take time. So if you explore one of these expect it to take months to up to a year. Also be prepared to have to explain your project in exhausting detail.

If you live in Canada, then you are in for some luck. You can try for the Independent Production Fund (IPF), a private fund based out of Toronto and Montreal that since 2010 has been funding scripted series for the web and mobile platforms. It has funded shows like *Ruby Skye P.I.*, *Guidestones*, and *Prison Dancer* with financing from $50,000 to $150,000. But, it must be a Canadian series from a Canadian producer and the series must be scripted with a narrative arc. The IPF also runs the Wip portal which features Canadian web series (wipwebseries.ca). So if you have a brand new series you need funding for that seems to fit that criterion, then click on over to the IFP and see if they may be able to invest in your show: http://ipf.ca/IPF/

If you live in the United Kingdom you can take a look at the British Film Institute (BFI), a charitable organization established by Royal Charter. In 2011 it took over lottery funding for film from the now abolished UK Film Council's lottery programme. The UK documentary series *The Specials* was partially funded by this. The series won two Webby Awards in 2010. That lottery programme was absorbed into the BFI Film Fund. http://www.bfi.org.uk/

If you live in France you can seek support from the Centre National du Cinema (CNC). In the past they have made available $3 million for helping finance web series. http://www.cnc.fr/web/en

There are a number of similar grants in America. If your program is educational and/or documentary then take a look at grants from organizations like the John D and Catherine T MacArthur Foundation and Alfred P Sloan Foundation. Another option is the Public Media Content Fund which in 2013 backed nine film programs, including two web series. The grants ranged from $5,000 to $100,000 for various genres and are for (quoted from their website) "... any subject that relates to or is representative of Latino Americans that is appropriate for public television and/or one of its platforms." You can find more information at Latino Public Broadcasting — http://www.lpbp.org/

Pitching to a Studio or Distributor

Pitching to a network or television studio is nearly impossible without an agent. But these studios can spend less on web series so there is more willingness to take chances. Syfy Channel has Syfy Digital and Warner Brothers has Warner Premiere Digital. You can also pitch to online-only production companies like Machinima, Maker Studios, Fullscreen, and Vuguru. You can also pitch to online distribution platforms that commission original programming like Crackle and My Damn Channel.

The stories of how these deals are made can vary from traditional pitches to the odd tale of *Mercury Men*. This pulp black-and-white sci-fi web series created by Chris Preksta was picked up by Syfy digital and it all started with a simple tweet from Craig Engler of Syfy Channel to Preksta, "hey I saw your tweet about the trailer, can I take a look at it?" You just never know what will open up doors.

When pitching to any of these options you'll want the same type of paperwork as you would for an investor. Since they may be taking a chance on you, the more you can show the better. You may want to make a sizzler reel or proof-of-concept episode. I would also suggest showing your social media following if it is substantial. Sorry, your work starts well before the pitch, much like crowdfunding campaigns do.

Funded. Check.

I've covered a lot of funding options and as you can tell I put a lot of time in crowdfunding. It is one of the best ways for a web series creator to gain funding early in their career, but there is no doubt that working with investors or a studio or distributor can provide you the funds for a high quality series. But keep in mind that the ones who control the funds can also control the story, so if you go that route make sure you are okay with making changes based on the desires of others in charge of the money. Many young creators will gladly make that sacrifice to jump-start their careers, while others resist what they consider compromising their creative vision. Either way, good luck and I hope you find the money you need to make your dream a reality.

Suggested Reading

You can write an entire book on funding a web series or film. Heck, some writers already have. If you need more information on funding, look into the following books for more information.

Crowdfunding for Filmmakers: The Way to a Successful Film Campaign
by John T. Trigonis

The Art of Film funding – 2nd Edition
by Carole Lee Dean

Shaking The Money Tree – 3rd Edition
by Morrie Warshawski

Selling Your Story in 60 Seconds
by Michael Hauge

CHAPTER 4

THE QUEST FOR TALENT

"If you don't have good actors, forget it."
— Yuri Brown, creator/actress *Cursed*

Web series creation and film-making as a whole is truly a collaborative effort. Unless this is a one-person show all done with selfies, you are going to need actors to bring your show to life. And no matter how talented you are, even if you have mastered the art of operating the camera, directing, and holding a boom pole at the same time, your project will be better off with talented crew members. Not only will you be less stressed, but the final product will be stronger because each person you bring in has the potential to invigorate a piece of the puzzle that is your show.

A talented actor will bring depth to a character in a way you could have never imagined and a skilled director of photography can elevate the cinematography to a true art form of award-winning video. Never underestimate the value of an excellent cast and crew ... or the terrible destruction a bad cast and crew can cause. So you better work hard to find the right talent behind and in front of the camera to make your show a success.

Easier said than done, right? If you are new to filmmaking, you may not know how to find cast and crew. Even locally you may not be sure where to start. So let's cover some of the ways you can find them.

Casting Director: If you have money, then you'll likely want to hire a casting director (or bribe with brownies one you are friends with) to help you find actors. If they are experienced they will already know where to look for the talent you need and will take a large load of the work off of you. But, that is if you have money to even afford one. Casting director rates can vary greatly.

So, saying you do need to find one. One good way is to use IMDb Pro to look at who cast projects in your genre. Casting directors often specialize in certain genres (comedies, sci-fi/fantasy, etc.), so to get the best bang out of your buck you'll want to find someone that specializes in your genre.

Another option is to click on over to the Casting Society of America website (http://www.castingsociety.com) where you can post about your project and attempt to get a CSA member to apply. And don't fret, if that accomplished casting director is just way too expensive, then reach out to their casting associates or assistants who may be willing to work for far less to get the additional experience.

Now if you don't have the money to pay a casting director, then you are going to have to do the leg work. So, let's look at some options for finding cast and while we are at it, because some of these options work for both, let's seek out crew too.

1. Theaters

Even though you may be looking for actors to act in front of the camera, you may be surprised by excellent actors on the stage. Some may already be dabbling in acting on camera and others may be wanting to try it out. If you don't have any connections to local theaters, then it is time to make them. If you are an actor, then audition for a play. You will quickly learn who some of the other actors are in the area. If not an actor, no worries. Just attend shows. After the show is over, go up to actors that especially impressed you and chat with them. Talk to them about your filmmaking and how you think they might be great for a part in a future production, then give them your business card (please tell me you have one). Even better, if things are going well, try to get their contact information so you can contact them directly to let them know about any auditions.

Although stage actors may need some tweaking for acting on camera, these actors are often very passionate about their craft. If you see a fantastic performance on stage, then there is potential there for a brilliant performance for your show.

2. Colleges & Schools

Take a look at your local colleges and schools, especially if you have film schools near you. Often they have acting programs and if you contact them they may promote a casting call for your production. Sometimes universities can be protective of the time of their students and may not be friendly toward them working on non-school programs, but depending on the school program and the time of the year (summers are often great), then you just might luck out and get some excellent young actors auditioning for your project.

3. Organizations

There are many excellent organizations that can help you spread the word about your casting and crewing call.

- The International Academy of Web Television (http://iawtv. org): The IAWTV has an active Facebook group for members. You can use this to reach potential cast and crew who you know are already familiar with the web television format.

- Independent Web Series Creators of Canada (http://iwcc-ciwc. org/): The IWCC (in their words) "...exists to support, encourage and promote independent, audience focused, creator driven web series, primarily in Canada but also around the world." You don't have to be from Canada, although you will find the organization more helpful if you are. They offer networking opportunities and will promote you on their social media sites, both of which could help you get cast and crew if you live in Canada.

4. Craigslist

Yes, you can post more on Craigslist (http://www.craigslist.org) than just furniture you want to get rid of. You can use it as a simple and free way to spread the word about your production. It works better in larger cities. Warning: The experience level of actors or crew will vary wildly with this method, but will expand your reach.

5. Facebook Groups

There are entire Facebook groups out there just for casting and/or crew calls. This can be an excellent way to cast a wide net and get attention for the project. Just search for them on Facebook and you'll find some with a little digging. If you live in a city with any filmmaking the chances are good there will also be a local group.

6. LinkedIn

Probably not one of my first choices, but if you have a large network of filmmaking friends on LinkedIn, then you may be able to search through their contacts to find possible actors or crew.

7. Film Commissions

Film commissions are non-profit/public organizations that attempt to attract motion media production crews (for movies, TV, commercials, web series, etc.) to shoot on location in their respective area with the belief that by bringing productions to their area there will be direct economic benefit to the area. There are over 1,000 such organization around the world, primarily in the United States, Asia, and Europe. These film commissions often have great resources to offer including communicating casting or crew calls to filmmakers in the area. Check out the film commission in your area and see what resources they may be able to offer to help you find talent. Here is an excellent website that lists film commissions: http://filmcommissioners.com/

8. Talent Agencies

If you are trying to reach a high level of talent you'll need to reach out to talent agencies. Unless you are willing to pay for travel, you'll want to search for talent agencies in nearby cities. Send them your casting call and follow-up on the phone to make sure they are aware of your production. Different agencies will react differently, but if they have talent seeking projects to expand their reel or get greater exposure, then a web series may interest them.

9. Mandy & similar sites

Mandy (http://www.mandy.com) is a very popular website that posts crew gigs and casting notices. You can use it to find a job or post for cast and crew for your project. Another site similar to Mandy and also very popular is ProductionHUB (http://www.productionhub.com).

Some large sites where you can post casting calls are Backstage (http://www.backstage.com), Casting Networks (http://home.castingnetworks.com), and Breakdown Express (http://www.breakdownexpress.com).

An excellent social media version is Stage 32 (http://www.stage32.com). It is a sort of Facebook meets LinkedIn for those in film. Still relatively new, it can be a good way to meet cast and crew. You can post projects or seek out people by what job roles they list themselves under.

Spidvid (http://www.spidvid.com) is a site that allows you to post video projects and accept bids from people who want to fill roles you are looking for.

There are countless other sites online that operate like these sites, but these are some of the ones I've used in the past.

10. Getting a "Name" Attached

It is no secret that by getting a "name" actor you can get a boost in your series. Not only more viewers, but more press coverage and possibly new investors. But how do you get them? Well, first network ... like a lot. While you are doing that build your cred by making some smaller projects. A well-known actor is rarely going to take a chance on a first-time filmmaker. So you need to do some work to build up your credibility.

Then, have a darn good script. No matter what you do, if your script is flawed then it is a sure thing that the actor will say no at some point. So make sure that script offers a great story and gives the actors an awesome meaty part that he or she will enjoy. Something a little different than they normally get to play is usually a great choice.

Now, you've built some contacts, I'm assuming you've been headhunting (aka watching lots of TV and movies) to help you pick out actors you want. Now I would suggest getting an IMDb Pro account. You can use this account to look up your actor choices and get their agent or manager contacts. Remember that networking? Well, hopefully you'll make a contact that will help you get around the agents, but if that fails then you can use IMDb Pro to contact them. You need to be ready to pitch your amazing and cleverly written series that has a gifted crew that will bring it to life ... you know the series that will open the actor up to a new audience. Time to put on that salesperson hat and sell your project to the actor's agent. No matter what, you'll have to pay them something, but if you pitch well, have a good script, their schedule doesn't conflict, you offer enough money, and the stars align then you just might snag a name actor. You'll want them to sign a Letter of Interest (LOI) to help secure them enough to start promoting them. That doesn't guarantee they won't leave later if something better paying happens, but it helps solidify that commitment. Of course, if you already have the money and dates locked you can just have them sign a real contract, but this is the option if that isn't the case.

You don't just want any name actor either. You want one that makes sense for your target audience. Sci-fi fans will love a former *Star Trek* actor, while soap fans may not give a care. Plus, you ideally want a name that is also social media savvy. They can help promote your series, which could be well worth any money you are paying them. And this is where the so-called web celeb, or YouTuber/web series star can come in handy. They are easier and cheaper usually to get, plus usually with a large social media base. Their fanbase may not be helpful for a traditional television series, but they could be huge for a web series, since they already consume their entertainment there. So don't ignore the web celeb, they may end up being the biggest "name" of them all for your show.

Oh, and if they are experienced, you will almost surely have to deal with SAG-AFTRA.

11. SAG-AFTRA New Media contracts

At some point you'll want to become a SAG signatory producer so you can work with SAG-AFTRA actors. The process isn't too hard, but it does take time. You should turn in your SAG signatory paperwork at least two weeks before the shoot. The paperwork is available online. You'll have to tell the union what the project is, how it will be distributed, and give a budget breakdown. They want to make sure you are sharing the money with the actors, which is fair especially if those actors are really talented and professional. Under the new media contract you have a lot of flexibility on the amount you can pay. If the budget is low enough the amount can be zero, not that I would suggest paying nothing if he or she is a good union actor; then a little money (if you have it) will be worth it. Also keep in mind that you will be required to pay Pension and Health contributions on top of whatever you pay in salary. At the time of this writing the rate is 16.5%.

12. WGA New Media contracts

After the infamous 2007–08 Writers Guild of America strike the WGA developed new media guidelines and contracts. Just as the SAG-AFTRA new media contract allows you to use actors for a fair rate, so to do these contracts. You can go to www.wga.org for more information and up-to-date contracts. It isn't necessary if you don't have a WGA member writing in the production, but if you are ever unsure what a proper writing credit would be, I would suggest using them as a guide.

13. Family & Friends

Surround yourself with talented friends who like film and you'll always have someone to ask to jump in front of or behind the camera. You always want to get the best actors and crew you can, but when all else fails you can ask a crew member to jump in for a small part (it happens all the time) or teach a friend how to adjust lights.

"Don't take advantage of your cast and crew. Don't disrespect them or treat them poorly. If you are going to have a bunch of people work for you for nothing or next to it, you are on their time so you respect them 100%." — Thomas Gofton, creator of *Mind's Eye*

Selecting Crew

Let's say you've spread the word, now you need to figure out who you want to add to your cast and crew. For crew it is a little easier. You see what past experience they have compared to others, talk to them to get a read on their personality to see if you want to work with them, and you check any references to see if they are reliable.

Finding out if they have the right experience is the easy part; the hard part is figuring out if they will clash with others in the crew. I've found it easy in productions to gauge skill based on reels, resumes, and an interview. The wild card is if they will show up on time and work hard. References will help weed out some; otherwise you'll just have to do a more extensive interview and try to get a read on how passionate they are for the project. If you can't pay much then you need to know they are doing it because they care about the project. I'll take ten inexperienced crew members who are truly passionate for the series over one extremely skilled crew member who doesn't care and will "phone it in," or worse, be a negative influence on the set. Personally, I prefer my drama on the page and on the screen, not on the set.

Selecting Cast

For actors you'll want to hold auditions. I always record auditions to view later to help me with narrowing down actors. Having the director(s), producer(s), and writer(s) there can be a great help to get feedback on performances and help make the right choices. The actor may do a cold read of sides from the script and/or do a monologue picked out by you or them. Keep them short at first, so you can have time to see a large number of actors. You are looking for a few things with actors:

- What their acting range or scope is.
- How well they take adjustments to their performance.

- Their screen presence. Does their charisma come across the screen?

- Are there any red flags with how they speak to you? Do they seem to care about this production and do they seem to respect you? Are they excited about the project?

- Do they add something to the character? The best actors will bring something new to characters that makes them even stronger.

You've Got Your Talent

Now you've got your cast and crew. Just remember Thomas Gofton's words of advice to me, don't take advantage of your cast and crew. They are likely working for this project for a reduced rate or for free, so keep that in mind and treat them with respect. Hopefully, everyone will work out and remember if they don't ... a character could die ... or magically have their face changed ... you get the idea.

Suggested Reading

There are not a lot of books out there on casting or finding crew. Below are a few books I found helpful that either had tips on casting or at the very least provided tips on how to work with actors and crew on set.

Directing Actors
by Judith Weston

I'll Be in My Trailer
by John Badham and Craig Modderno

Casting Revealed
by Hester Schell

CHAPTER 5

SPREADING THE WORD

Your Marketing Plan

I've already spoken a little about how you must market and need to know your audience. But I can't stress enough how crucial this is for the success of your web television project. You can make the greatest story in the world, but the old "build it and they will come" philosophy doesn't work anymore on the Internet. A few years ago you could create buzz by just being one of the first web series, but now there are hundreds of web series being made every year and it is very easy for your project to never get attention.

So how can we prevent that from happening? You come up with a marketing plan. You schedule it out, build your fanbase, spread the word, etc. You take that core audience we talked about in Chapter 1 and build on it. I'll take you through the various steps of things you can do to help your potential fans find you.

Creating Your Website

I sometimes get asked whether or not a web series creator should make a website. The short answer: yes. No matter how involved you are in social media, your website acts as the central hub of everything related to your web series. It makes it easier for people to find the series using a search engine and quickly follow the project on any social media platforms you spotlight on the page.

If you have more than one project, you can either make a separate page for each or (if they appeal to the same core audience) have them share a website. There are a few key things you should do on your website:

- Don't make them hunt for your video player. Make sure your video player is front and center. Have basic information about the series and if possible have a playlist so viewers can easily find the first episode or the newest. You don't want them wasting time trying to figure out what your show is and how to play the episode they want to see. I get so frustrated sometimes when I go to a web series website and it plays on default the most recent episode and I have to hunt to find the first episode. Don't make this mistake.

- Site navigation must be easy. Make it easy for new visitors to find information on what the series is about, who the cast are, who the crew are, where to watch the episodes, etc. Don't try to be overly creative on the navigation and confuse potential new fans.

- Prominently display your social media platforms. Make it easy for them to start following the series on Facebook, Twitter, etc. Also make it easy to find an email newsletter subscription on the site.

Sounds easy right? Well, if you don't have much experience on making websites then there may be some challenges for you. Try to get whoever is on your team with the most web design experience to build the site. But there are some easy ways now online to make sites with minimal knowledge. But if you are ever in doubt try to hire a web designer. Perhaps you can find a good one who will be excited enough by the project to work on it for free or cheap. Here are some steps on making your own website:

1. U R Your URL — Buy a Unique Domain Name: You want to snap up that domain name as soon as you have your title figured out. Try to make it as close to the title of the series as possible. Sometimes this won't be possible because the name is already taken. So you can then modify it if needed by adding "theseries,"

"series," "watch," or some other combination. The .com address is the most popular choice, but you could choose .TV or another to make it more unique. But most likely it is in your best interest to claim the .com address in addition to any other addresses.

2. Pick a Hosting Service: So now you have your domain name, but where are you going to have it point to? You want to pick a service that is fast and reliable. Do some price hunting and look at reviews online. It should go without saying that you want to find a service based in your own country. Not only does it cause you less of a headache if you need to contact them, not needing to wrestle with time zones and other issues, but it helps with Search Engine Optimization (SEO) because search engines tend to push to the top sites in the same country thinking they are more likely what a searcher is looking for.

3. Select Your CMS: Now you have a domain name and a place to host the site, but how are you going to create the actual site? This is where CMS or Content Management Systems comes in very handy, especially if you have limited HTML/CSS/JavaScript experience. These type of systems allow you to create, publish, and manage your content on the site in a far easier way with limited knowledge of HTML and the like. Three of the major kinds are WordPress, Drupal, and Joomla. I have the most experience with WordPress and it is by far the easiest of the three. It started more as a blogging software, but with updates allows great flexibility. Most hosting services will make it easy for you to download a CMS and get started. You can also turn to easy to set-up sites like Wix (www. wix.com) and Webs (www.webs.com).

4. Design the Site: One of the things I like most from WordPress is the wide number of free or inexpensive themes or templates that allow you to customize the site to look the way you want. There are a lot to choose from. You can go to WordPress.org to search for free themes or go to sites like ThemeForest (http:// themeforest.net) to find a wide selection of themes or templates that start as low as $3. Don't snatch up the first one you see though, do some digging and find your top picks. Make sure it will allow the streamlined navigation you need for visitors, is SEO friendly, and has a responsive design making it mobile-user friendly. If it isn't WordPress, then you will have a harder job of designing the site, but with a little knowledge (or help) you can accomplish the same goals.

5. Add a Blog: You don't have to add a blog, but it is a good way to build a rapport with your audience that allows you to go more in-depth than a tweet or a Facebook post. This is another place where WordPress excels since being a blog platform was its original goal. But all CMS can be used to create blogs and if you have built a static site from scratch you can still add a CMS just for the blog section if you wish. Blogs are also great for search engine optimization, helping drive an audience to your site. Plus, it allows your fans to comment back to you. You'll find blogging can create a conversation with your audience which is a great way to build a loyal fanbase. Each blog post doesn't have to be just text though; you can embed videos too. And you could have guest bloggers from the cast or crew. Be creative, blog often.

6. Add Email Subscriptions: I can't stress enough how important building an email list can be for your marketing. Make sure you include an email subscription box on your site. The traditional and safest place to put this is the upper right section of the website. Don't abuse your list and you will quickly build a fantastic and powerful way to communicate to your fans.

7. Add Social Media Links: Being on Twitter, Facebook, Tumblr, etc. isn't enough. You need an easy way for viewers to find your accounts on these social media platforms. Make sure you have them easy to find on your website. You can do this by adding a row of social media icons on the sites making it just one easy click for your fans to find you on their favorite social media platform. Two other popular social media tools you can add to your page in addition to the social media icons are a Facebook "Like" box and a Twitter feed. They are both easy enough to add using embedded coding that can be found on the official websites.

8. Get Analytical: Having a website is only so good if you don't know who is visiting it and where they are coming from. After seeing what keywords people are using to find you or seeing what websites they are coming from can be crucial tools to help you fine-tune your website or find new niche audiences to reach out to. There are many analytical tools available. Most hosts will have some kind of basic one included, but you should get something better. There are a few excellent options: Google Analytics (www.google.com/analytics/), Clicky (http://clicky.com), and Woopra (https://www.woopra.com). Google Analytics is easily the most popular one and all you need is a Google account to start using it. But analytics is its own art form, so be sure to do you homework on the best ways to use the tool.

Search Engine Marketing

Creating your website is great, but unless interested folks know your domain name or find you from one of your social media platforms, you need to help new potential audience members to find your series. That is where search engines come in.

There are two types of search engine marketing: **organic** and **paid**. Paid search engine marketing is paying to have your site featured for certain searches. This type of pay per click advertising is pretty straightforward and can help you find new audiences. But, if you are an independent filmmaker then most likely money is limited. That is where organic searches come into play.

Organic Search Engine Optimization (Organic SEO) is building a keyword strategy that will enable you to pull in audience members by getting your site placed on organic search engine results pages (SERPs) that your potential viewer will be looking for. What does that mean in English? It is creating a strategy that will help ensure that if a family member, friend, or some other person that has either heard of your project or is searching for projects with the same themes will find your site near the top. Got vampires in your show? You need to build a strategy to improve your chances of showing up on a search engine search if someone is looking for a web series about vampires. This type of search engine marketing is 100% free, but requires planning and some work. Luckily there are many tools now that help make it easier.

There are two types of keywords: head terms and long tail terms. Head terms are broad single word keywords like "vampire."

While long tail terms are longer and more narrow, for example, "vampire young romance sparkle." Yuck, now that is a horror story. Put yourself in the shoes of someone who in passing heard about your series and is now trying to find it online. Or those of someone that your show would be perfect for and figuring out what kind of narrow searches they might be making that could lead them to you. Those long tail terms are obviously the harder ones to figure out, but it is very important because 70% of searches are long tail. Also, because they are so narrow, the chances are much higher that someone finding your site using the search will be converted into a fan and join your growing audience.

So, how do you figure them out? One basic way is to start plugging keywords into the Google search engine and see what the auto-complete pulls up. For example, if I enter "Vampire" I get as options for long tail terms: Vampire Diaries, Vampire Academy, Vampire Diaries Season 5, and Vampire Weekend. Hmm... no sparkle but you can see a trend in vampire projects right now. Anyway, you can use this experiment with different phrasing to come up with ideas not only for keywords but also to find where your potential audience goes online.

You can also use various free or inexpensive keyword tools online:

- You can use Google Adwords to help you pick keywords — https://adwords.google.com/
- Wordstream's Keyword Tool — http://www.wordstream.com/keywords
- Wordtracker's Free Keyword Tool — https://freekeywords.wordtracker.com
- SEM Rush (paid tool with excellent free option) — www.sem-rush.com

So you need to come up with a list of keywords and apply them strategically on your website, press releases, and blog posts. Note, if you are using WordPress as your CMS you have lots of plug-in options that will help you with adding SEO to your website.

To help you also narrow down terms and find your core audiences you can use Google Trends (http://www.google.com/trends) to see how popular the terms are, how they trend over time, and what countries the terms are popular in.

Here are a few things to keep in mind for where to place keywords:

❶ Put keywords in the actual body of the web site. There are no hard rules on how many times a keyword can be repeated on the same page, but don't get too crazy with it. Usually it is suggested 2-4 times at the most depending on how long the page is.

❷ Be sure to put keywords in the title tags for each unique page of your website. Also while you are at it, put keywords in the Meta description tags, meta keyword tags, and Header tags of each web page.

❸ Be sure to change the file name of each image so it has a real name with keywords; instead of 1234.jpg you have FeliciaDayIsKevinBacon.jpg ... or something like that. Also use the <alt> image tags to put in descriptions that will help search engines know what those images are.

Press

You need to reach out to the press both offline and online. To do so you'll need to send out press releases, reach out to press contacts, and make a press kit.

1. Press Releases – The old school press release still lives, but should only be used for general releases. Save personal emails for the top writers and editors of blogs, news sites, and podcasts. So of course it helps if you are familiar with their work to better fine tune those emails to prove to them your news deserves coverage and would appeal to their audience. A few tips for generic press releases include:

● **Don't Bury Your Lead** – Don't fill your release with information that isn't key to the particular news you are trying to share. Work key points into the headline and subhead, making sure to repeat those points in the first paragraph. Journalists get a lot of press releases, so make sure you capture their attention quickly and impart the most important information right out of the gate.

- **Easy To Read** – Sadly, nowadays no one can read something without lots of white space breaking things up ... except for you because you're reading this book. But for everyone else, make sure you make it scannable friendly. Keep it under one page, use bullet points, use lists, and link to more information about your production company rather than taking up space with an About section.

- **Choose Your Subject Line Wisely** — The subject line of your email is the first they will see, so be careful not to make some common mistakes. Be clear, don't make it too long (4 or 5 words max), and don't use spam words that might get your email thrown into a spam folder or just be ignored by the journalist who gets a bad impression. Avoid words like Free, Sex, Make Money, Buy, etc. Oh, and don't USE ALL CAPS... that is just ANNOYING.

When you send out the generic press release you can use third party email services like MailChimp, which helps you make it look professional and track if it was ever opened. Post it on your website and share it via all of your social media networks. You can also use a wire service. It will help improve chances that it will get picked up by larger news aggregator sites like Google News and News 360. You can also send a press release out with free or inexpensive online press release distribution services like PRWeb (www.prweb.com) or PRLog (http://www.prlog.org). It is unlikely to get picked up much via those types of services, but at the very least it will create one or more inbound links to your site.

2. Press Kit/Press Room - Don't make it hard for people to promote your project and find out all the newsworthy information they need to know about the series. Be sure to create a Press section on the website. I know as a podcast host and entertainment news writer I love it when I find a web series website that has a good press page. So, please make it easy on us and make one. It should have all press releases collected (HTML, not pdf, so journalists can copy and paste text easier), promotional images (high-res and low-res pictures, artwork, and behind-the-scene photos), trailers (both embed YouTube video and downloadable HD video for press to play on TV), and complete contact information. And, of course, don't forget your press kit. This is usually a downloadable pdf. It should include your series tag line, synopsis (short with less than 100 words and long at more than 500 words), cast and crew bios, producer/director statement(s), production information, a feature story, reviews, and third party endorsements. Also, post as much of this information as possible in HTML on your site so can more easily be copied and pasted by a busy journalist.

Media Contacts

So where do you send your snazzy press release, ask for reviews, or line up interviews? Here is a list of media contacts you can reach out to. I would suggest checking them out before you reach out. See what their articles, podcasts, or web casts are like. See if your show would appeal to them and learn enough about them so you can customize your messages to them. Remember, there are people behind each of these sites and they get contacted every day by people just like you. To stand out, it helps if you can demonstrate that you know their show and tailor a message for them.

News Sites/Bloggers

(Web Series Specific)

British Web Series – Another blog done by Elisar Cabrera which collects links to different British web series. If your series is British then it is a good blog to contact.
http://britishwebseries.blogspot.co.uk/

Digital Chick TV – Created in 2010 by writer/director/producer Daryn Strauss, Digital Chick TV is a blog and web community focused on the contributions of women in web series either in front of and/or behind the camera.
   http://digitalchicktv.com/

New Media Rockstars — Founded in December of 2011, NMR is an online magazine which does coverage and analysis of new media content.
http://newmediarockstars.com/

Slebisodes - Founded in October 2009 by Patrick Bardwell, this online magazine focuses on web series. The site is an online program guide for web series, news articles, tips on making web series, and has a daily calendar.
http://slebisodes.com

Snobby Robot — Founded by Erik Urtz, this online trade-style magazine is dedicated to the web series community. It covers reviews of web series, showcases creators, and offers tips on how to make your own web series.
http://snobbyrobot.com/

Televisual — Televisual investigates the present and future of television, with a focus on web television. The site has been quoted by major mainstream news sites like *The New York Times* and *Vanity Fair*.
http://blog.ajchristian.org/

Tubefilter — Tubefilter is an online news website focused on web television. The site does reviews, news, and interviews. Based in Los Angeles with offices in New York, they created the Streamy Awards and host web television creator meet-ups at the Tubefilter Hollywood Meetup.
http://www.tubefilter.com

Web Series Channel — Besides being a site that allows access to a wide range of series, it also has news and does interviews.
http://www.webserieschannel.com

Web Series Today — This web series blog (using Blogger) is an "open collaborative community-based blog." You can submit news to them, but also request to join the blog as a contributor. As a contributor you can post news or your newest episodes. They also have their own Google+ Community.

(Not Web Series Specific)
Her Film Project — This website/blog supports women filmmakers and helps to share their experiences in film.

http://www.herfilmproject.com

Pinkray Gun — Since February 2007, Pinkray Gun has considered itself the antidote to the stereotypical fansite by offering a platform for geeks, fans, and creators who they feel are traditionally under-represented in science fiction, fantasy, horror, and comics. The site leans towards woman creators or shows that appeal to women, but they do welcome both genders.

http://www.pinkraygun.com/

ScifiPulse — I often write for this website. For years ScifiPulse has been covering science fiction/fantasy news and doing interviews. Mostly they cover a wide range of mediums including TV shows, movies, comic books, and video games. They often cover sci-fi web series.

Slacktory — This comedic blog is about the pop culture of the Internet. It's a part of the My Damn Channel Blog Network.

http://www.slacktory.com/

Splitsider — This site focuses on comedy in movies, TV shows, books, and (you guessed it) web series.

http://splitsider.com

TVline — The site does bi-weekly web series recommendations.

http://tvline.com/category/web-series/

Podcasts

GenreTainment — A podcast that I co-host with Julie Hernandez Seaton. We interview writers, producers, directors, actors, etc. We don't focus exclusively on web series, but we often do interview web series creators.

http://GenreTainment.com

Indie Intertube — April Grant and Amanda Shockley interview web series creators, have their own yearly awards they hand out, and often speak about web series news.

http://indieintertube.tv/

Limited Release — Out of Canada, Nick Montgomery and Candice Lepage do reviews on web series and occasionally chat about web series news.

http://limitedreleasepodcast.ca/

Surfing Aliens — Tim Keaty and co-host(s) interview a creator from a different web series in each episode.
http://surfingaliens.com

Web Chats

Super Geeked Up — Web series creator Jeff Burns (*Super Knocked Up*) hosts this Google Hangout live web chat having guests on each week from different web series. Jeff inserts a lot of humor and inter-activity with fans on Twitter.
http://superknockedup.com/episodes/super-geeked-up/

Web Series Watch — Cindy Marie Jenkins and Patty Jean Robinson are always looking for guests and web series topics to discuss on their web chats.
http://web-series-watch.com

What Is Your Klout?

Besides hearing back from your audience and the number of fans, followers, or whatever you want to call them, it is hard to know if you are being successful in your marketing online. If only there was a score telling you how awesome you are.

What, there is? There are a number of social influence tools that claim to measure online influence. The only one I have a lot of experience with and hear mentioned much in connection to web series is Klout. But it is far from the only one. Find one that you like and use it to check in and see how things are going. The higher your score, the more influential you are in the social media, or at least that is the idea. Keep in mind these aren't always 100% accurate, so take them with a grain of salt. Here are the top ones: Klout (http://klout.com), PeerIndex (http://peerindex.com), Kred (http://kred.com), TwitterGrader (http://twittergrader.mokumax.com), and Wefollow (http://wefollow.com).

Courting Influencers

The Internet is full of "influencers," people that different niche audiences listen to. They could be celebrities, politicians, bloggers, critics, actors, artists, musicians, community leaders, podcasts, etc.

You want to find influencers that speak to the niche audiences you hope to reach early on in the development of your project.

Start at the top finding the most popular. You can do searches and look at who is blogging or writing news stories in these fields. You can get help from a news aggregation site like AllTop.com to help you find bloggers covering your niche. You can also use Twitter to find influencers, which Followerwonk (https://followerwonk.com) can help greatly with. Once you identify influencers, try to build a relationship with them in someway before reaching out to let them know about your series and asking for their support via a review, interview, or in some other way.

Felicia Day: The Kevin Bacon of Web Television

I mention writer/actress Felicia Day a lot in this book. She is without a doubt one of the most well-known web series celebs from the early days of web series (you know, a couple of years ago). I kid that she is the Kevin Bacon of web television because she is connected to so many different web series creators or series. Between her creation of *The Guild*, the founding of the YouTube channel *Geek & Sundry*, starring in *Dr. Horrible's Sing-Along Blog*, and a million guest appearances she is everywhere. She is one of the top influencers in web series and geekdom. If you manage to get her attention, an endorsement would be huge, but don't count on it. She is busy doing the work of ten mortal web series creators. But seriously, I mean she has (just clicked over) a Klout score of 88, which is the exact same score of ... Kevin Bacon. Do I need any more proof?

Social Media Marketing

Social media marketing is an excellent way to pull in new people to join your audience. Once they are pulled in, social media allows you to build relationships to develop a deeper connection with your audience so they stick around. You'll also find it helps pull in people via organic search engine use, not just whatever social media network you are using.

Remember, as soon as you secure that domain name, you should click on over to Know Em (http://knowem.com) or Check

Usernames (http://checkusernames.com) to see if your username is free over hundreds of social media platforms. Then go forth and secure! You want to try and make that username as consistent as possible between platforms.

80/20 Rule

Don't forget the 80/20 Rule of marketing. It is crucial in social media. No one likes someone that only talks about themselves, especially over and over and over again. Mix it up. Offer other content and sneak in links to your series or other news for your project. For example, on Twitter I do a #Crowdfunding and #Webseries picks of the day. I find ones that I think should be spotlighted. The creators appreciate it and I feel like I'm offering something useful to my followers. I also often post inspirational quotes (people love quotes in social media). These are all very simple things for me to do and keep up with. It makes it so I'm promoting or contributing useful information 80% of the time and 20% of the time talking about my actual product (web series, merchandise, crowdfunding campaign, film, etc.). That 80% also includes conversations with followers/fans too. Don't forget to interact and be ... social.

I'm going to list some of the top social media platforms you should be on, including some tips. You'll find that social media can eat up a lot of time. Your best bet is to limit yourself to the top three where your core audience are located. If you can, try to get a team of people working with you to manage the social media platforms. What are generally the top choices? Facebook, Twitter, and Google+ are three top ones. In the end though, it depends on where your core audience hangs out. Perhaps they are very visual with pictures and you will find a huge following on Pinterest, or you'll find that on YouTube your audience is huge in interacting with you. There are hundreds of social media platforms, so there are many possibilities. Let's take a look at some of the top choices.

Facebook

Facebook was founded in February 2004 by Mark Zuckerberg and his friends Eduardo Saverin, Andrew McCollum, Dustin Moskovitz and Chris Hughes. Facebook is one of the most popular social media websites with over 1.11 billion (March 2013) users. And according to Pew Research Center surveys, 57% of all American adults and 73% of all those ages 12–17 use Facebook. So it can be a useful tool for spreading the word about your web series.

Sadly, Facebook is not as useful as it once was. Ever since introducing its paid advertising platform, page engagement has fallen incredibly fast. How much does it effect your reach? In February of 2012 Facebook told businesses that an average of only 16% of the members on their business page actually get exposed on their newsfeed to the content that they upload. Your own personal page still reaches your friends fairly well, sort of, but an official page for your series/film will do horrible. You'll notice as the followers grow that your posts will reach less and less of the percentage of overall followers. Many web series creators have become frustrated, especially starting in 2014. The only option you have to keep certain posts reaching a large portion of your followers on your page is Promoted Posts, which lets Facebook page owners pay a flat rate in order to have a single post reach a larger number of users and, in theory, increasing that specific post's reach and impressions.

But, some recent experiments have called in question how useful a paid promotion really is. One thing complicating matters are click farms. These companies have people click "like" for posts that they are paid to like. Some experiments have shown convincing evidence that these click farms are a heavy percentage of paid promoted posts on Facebook. Is Facebook paying click farms to click away? No, but click farms click things outside of what they are paid for to make it harder for social media companies to counter their efforts, hence they swoop in and click these promoted posts. Sure you get posts reaching more "people." But in reality many of them are not going to join your audience, so you end up wasting your hard-earned money promoting posts. Perhaps someday Facebook will fix this, but I wouldn't hold your breath. You'll need to decide to promote or not promote, but be aware of these issues when you make that choice for certain posts.

With that said, you still need to be on Facebook. You'll reach some people and it is expected for you to have a presence on Facebook. Below are a few tips.

Facebook Tips

1. Create an official Facebook page, but don't forget your personal page. If your personal page is exclusively ... well, personal, then you'll want to keep it separate. But if you mix business with pleasure on your Facebook page like a lot of web series creators, then you should make sure to post updates about your project on Facebook also. Personal pages tend to fair better in spreading updates to friends.

2. Get graphic with your posts. I don't mean NSFW (Not Suitable For Work) pictures or violent videos, but you're close. I do mean less text and more media. Facebook loves it when you use pictures or download videos. The social media network prioritizes videos and photos first, followed by links and status updates. So keep that in mind and make sure to post a lot of pictures and videos.

3. Invite your friends. When you make a business page for your project, but sure to invite all of your friends from your personal page. It is a great way to get your first followers.

4. Be social with your followers. Just like other social media networks, don't forget to reply to comments and interact as much as you can to any followers that interact with you.

Twitter

Created in March 2006, this microblogging platform allows users to send and read short 140-character text messages (aka Tweets). Who would have thought back then that such a simple concept would blow up into one of the largest social media platforms? According to Twitter's own statistics, in June 2013 Twitter had 218 million active users. Its growth in users per year could be faster, but there is no denying that it still has a huge following and there are plenty of case studies where marketing and even crowdfunding for films have been done successfully almost exclusively via Twitter, so it is obvious it can be a very useful tool for you if you learn how to use it.

You can create a personal Twitter account, a Twitter account for your series, Twitter account(s) for a fictional character, or a combination of them all. Obviously, the more accounts the more of a workload you are giving yourself. So be careful not to make it more complicated than you or your team can manage. If you have to choose only one, often a personal Twitter account is the best choice and you can share future projects with all of your followers moving forward.

Twitter Tips

1. Make it pretty — You want to create a custom header, background, and avatar pics. No one trusts or takes seriously accounts without original avatar pics at the very least. Show you are legit and make it visually easy for someone to spot your account.

2. Introduce Yourself – Make sure to fill out that bio with the project's description and make sure to sneak in a few of the keywords if you can.

3. Be Consistent – You want to make sure you tweet often. You don't have to be obsessively posting everyday, but ... it wouldn't hurt. On slow news days or busy days just one tweet during the day will fulfill that consistent goal. Managing and scheduling tweets will be a huge help and I'll talk more about that soon.

4. Build a Following – So how do you get more followers? There are many strategies. Let's look at a few:

- Follow Others: Find other people on Twitter that would be interested in your project. Other web series creators, web series news folks, fans of the genre you are doing, festivals, etc. Some will follow you back and others won't but they may have tweets that you can share with your other followers. Once you have followers you can see who they are following to help you find more people to follow ... just let it snowball and you will not only follow more, but soon see your own followers grow.

- Favorite Others: Sometimes just favoriting someone's tweet can cause them to follow you. Less likely than if you follow them, but it is a less-commitment option that is easy to do that might gain you some new followers.

- Tweet Chats: These type of live chats are done by everyone following the same hashtag at the same time and talking to each other. For example, the podcast Surfing Aliens does an #AlienLife chat while everyone listens to a new episode. It is a great way to bring that live event feel with something that would normally not have it. Another is #webserieschat (managed by Slebisodes and Mingle Media TV). These Twitter Chats give exposure to your series to influencers who are either leading the chat or participating, which could lead to building relationships with them. They also give opportunities for you to be quoted by bloggers or other media. Regular participation or leading a Twitter Chat increases your authority and can lead to invitations to speak publicly or other opportunities. You can use social platforms Twubs (http://twubs.com), TWChat (http://twchat.com), and TweetChat (http://tweetchat.com) to help find or organize Twitter Chats. I sometimes participate in Twitter Chats; they can be a lot of fun and will almost always snag a new follower or two. I would encourage you to try them out.

- Search For Followers: You can use the search on Twitter to seek certain keywords that could lead you to Twitter accounts that you should follow or at least interact with. There are also directories online that might help you find people to follow or interact with: Twellow (http://www.twellow.com) and Twibs (listing businesses on Twitter) http://www.twibs.com.

- Time for Lists: Once you start following a large number of accounts you'll need to manage them, otherwise you will spend the day on hunting for tweets to re-tweet. I would suggest making lists (they can be marked private if you want) of those you feel are high on your list of ones you follow that you think are great for re-tweeting to your followers. Make another list of those you want to interact with often to maintain a relationship, like journalists, bloggers, podcasters, festivals, distributors, and other web series creators.

- Manage Your Tweets: If you have more than one Twitter account, or your account becomes very large, you are going to need to come up with ways to manage it. You are in this biz to make series and films after all, not tweet all day. First off, you can use a social media tool like Hootsuite (http://hootsuite. com) or TweetDeck (http://tweetdeck.com/) to keep track of all of those tweets. I personally love Buffer (https://bufferapp. com) because it allows me to schedule tweets throughout the day. It is also useful in re-posting (with different wording) the same information on different times or days. It made a huge difference in my ability to get regular tweets out during the day, but don't go on auto-pilot. You still need to log-in occasionally and show you are a person by interacting with others. Oh, and tools like TwitterGrader (http://twittergrader.mokumax.com) and Twitalyzer (http://www.twitalyzer.com) are good ways to get a snapshot of how you are doing and perhaps figure out ways to improve your tweeting habits. Followerwonk (https:// followerwonk.com) is one of my favorite tools for analytics on followers and I love how it syncs with Buff to help me customize my scheduled tweets around the activity of my followers.

- Tweet More Than Text: People love it when you mix it up and tweet pictures, audio, or video. Some useful tools online that can help make it easier for you to do are: Twitpic (http:// twitpic.com), Yfrog (http://yfrog.com), and AudioBoo (http:// audioboo.fm).

Google+

Launched as an invitation-only field test on June 28, 2011, Google+ (Google Plus) is another social network that is similar to Facebook and is the second largest social networking site after Facebook. According to Google, who owns the platform in case you hadn't guessed, the network had 540 million active users in October 2013. Not bad, but still fairly far behind Facebook. But there are many reasons to be on Google+. Besides reaching out to an audience that may prefer this network over Facebook, it is also a huge help for your Search Engine Optimization Plan. The Google search engine is the most popular search engine and it shouldn't be a surprise that Google+ ranks really well in Google searches. It also does well on mobile. According to unofficial reports from GlobalWebIndex, it was used by 30% of smartphone users between April–June 2013. That makes it the fourth most used app.

Google+ has less people on it, but guess what? That means you have less voices to try to shout over to be heard. So if you can build followers in that network they will likely be more engaged, which means they are better fans who will support your series. I really think it is a powerful tool that is often ignored, but can be powerful gear in your overall marketing machine. Below are a few tips for you.

Google+ Tips

1. Introduce Yourself — Much like the other social media networks you need to make sure you do a good job filling out your profile. Make sure to add a good profile picture and cover picture, similar concepts that you used in Facebook and Twitter. The About page gives you great opportunities and far more flexibility than Twitter and arguably Facebook. Be sure to add information about your series and make these sections SEO-friendly with keywords worked in that are relevant for your medium and genre(s). You can also link to specific pages from this page, so be sure to link to your website and other important social media networks you are using. A really cool feature is that you can use bullets in your description. This allows you to create easy-to-read lists of your projects and/ or services.

2. Social+ — Don't be passive in Google+. Much like Twitter you have to be pro-active and socialize with other users to ever hope to build a following. Be sure to post often and make sure to seed posts with important keywords. Also make sure you comment often and +1 other's posts. Just like you, they are trying to build a following. Other web series creators love to support each other, but they have to find you first. So make it easy for them to know you are out there.

3. Google+ Events – A really useful tool for inviting people to see a new episode, invite fans to offline screenings, let people know about panel appearances, etc. The events feature allows Google+ users to send out customized invitations to anyone. Facebook has something similar, but what is cool is that this event tool can send it to people regardless of whether they are Google+ users. It also syncs up well with Google Calendar and shows up automatically after confirmation. You can also do Party Mode which allows everyone in attendance to upload pictures into the same album using the Google+ mobile app. Then using Google+ you can show the photos in chronological order like a slideshow. Oh, and it works really well with sending out invites for Google+ Hangouts.

4. Communities & Shared Circles – One of the best ways to build relationships and a following on Google+ is to join Communities. Be sure to interact with those fans of genres you are working on or with fellow professionals in your field. You can also add entire shared circles allowing to quickly follow other users that you think may find what you have to say interesting.

5. Google Hangouts – Perhaps one of the most powerful tools unique to Google+ is Google Hangouts. This tool lets you create live web chats with up to 10 people total, they just need cameras that can stream to the Internet and boom — instant communication. You can also share screens and take advantage of all types of little additional features. Not only is this just a useful tool to meet with other production teammates that may be across the country or world, but you can also use it as a big social media tool.

Hangouts on Air (HOA) allows you to take that video connection with up to 10 people and turn it into a live broadcast to an unlimited audience online. Once the HOA has ended it will automatically become a draft in your YouTube account where you can edit and then publish it. You can then share that URL or embed code anywhere online allowing you to extend your audience past just Google+.

An excellent example of a web series that took advantage of HOA is *Super Knocked Up*. Jeff, in an attempt to let his audience get to know his new lead actress, Jourdan Gibson, had her do HOAs, which morphed into a weekly HOA show called *Super Geeked Up* (notice he tied it to the brand name of his web series too). By having guests on every week from other web series, the show can promote those web series while also promoting Jeff's own web series. Since new audience members tuning in are likely fans of the web series' guest of the night, that means they already like the web series medium so they just may also be interested in Jeff's series. Plus, it helps him draw in new people that know about either his series or the guests, enhancing the marketing reach for everyone.

Jeff also uses Twitter Chats (see previous section on Twitter for more information) to help audience members ask questions and communicate with him, co-hosts and the guests. This takes the HOA to an even larger level of social interaction and can be a fantastic way to not only build your audience, but also just make the show more fun and dynamic.

Another example is the web series *Generic Girl*. Co-creator Victor Solis hosted a series of HOA specials called *Digital Spill* which had panels of experts or interviews with web series guests. This was done around the time that *Generic Girl* was first launching and was on the same channel on YouTube. It helped make *Generic Girl* much more well known and Solis was even quoted saying that it may have played the largest factor in their series being nominated for an IAWTV award, because it helped it go from obscurity to being in the minds of IAWTV members while voting for nominees. Now *Digital Spill* had a shorter life span than *Super Geeked Up*, so it is a good example of how you don't have to have a long-term weekly HOA to accomplish the same results. You could make it for a shorter run for just times around when you premiere and shortly after to help in building awareness and contacts in the web series community.

But what other ways can you use an HOA if you don't feel like making a talk show? You can also do a Q&A type of event. Allowing audience members a chance to ask questions to members in the crew or cast. This helps build a relationship with fans. You could also just do special HOAs for crowdfunding updates, quick behind-the-scenes chats about the series, running contests, etc.

Although doing an HOA is made to be SEO-friendly and gets you instant distribution on YouTube, you still should use a few tips to increase the chances of people stumbling on your videos. Make sure you have your keyword list handy and weave those keywords into the video conversation, into the title, and into the description text. Also make sure you use tags and include them in the video conversation. Another keyword-rich thing to do (but is time consuming) is to create a transcript of the video.

Once your HOA is done and published, follow the same type of tips you would for any YouTube video: add the video to a playlist, add annotations, and share that video across all of your social media networks.

YouTube

This extremely popular video-sharing site was founded in February 2005 by three former PayPal employees. In November 2006 Google bought YouTube for $1.65 billion. It is easily the largest video platform on the Internet and, less commonly known, it is the second largest search engine (after Google... who now owns YouTube... clever Google). The YouTube audience is enormous; according to YouTube's statistics there are more than 1 billion unique users visiting YouTube each month and there are over 6 billion hours of video being watched each month on YouTube with 100 hours of video being uploaded to YouTube every minute. And according to Nielsen studies, YouTube reaches more US adults ages 18-34 than any cable network. So it goes without saying that at some point you'll want your series on YouTube or at the very least promotional videos for your series. I don't know about you, but if I hear about a new show or movie and I want to look for a trailer I almost always try YouTube first. So be sure if someone decides to look your series up, they can find something.

Did I mention YouTube is very search-engine friendly, especially with Google? Forrester Research reported that videos are 53%

more likely than a traditional website to receive an organic first-page ranking in Google.

YouTube Tips

1. Customize Your Channel – Like the other social media network accounts, you need to flesh out your account and make it look attractive by adding pictures. You should also use a keyword-rich description with the http link to your website. Don't forget to link the account with your other social media networks. This channel should be for your web series, unless you have more than one project for your production, then you'll want to make this channel for your overall production company.

2. Make It Easy To Find – Don't make it hard for people searching YouTube. Besides the keywords in your description of the channel, you should also add relevant tags. You can use YouTube to help you figure these out by using YouTube Suggest which is that effect that happens when you start to enter a word in the YouTube search box and it starts auto-filling options. That gives you clues as to the top things people are searching on YouTube and can help you with those tags and keywords. You also want to build links. You can do that by encouraging viewers to rate the video or add a comment. You can accomplish this by either posting a video response to a popular video or by getting your video added to a popular playlist. You can also increase your ranking in search engines by getting external sites to link to your YouTube videos. This is where getting linked by blogs, news sites, etc. can be a huge help.

3. Schedule Wisely – View counts on YouTube are a gift and a curse. If your view count increases quickly it can generate more interest, thus attracting even more views. Sadly, it works both ways: If your view count stagnates it affects the perceived value of your video and some people will skip watching it or sharing it because of this. So when you schedule your video's premiere, be aware of this possible issue. Don't post your video at 8 pm in the evening. A YouTube "day" starts at midnight PST, so if you time your premiere soon after that you will truly get all day for it to build its first day of views.

4. Playlists Are Your Friend – YouTube playlists are a great way to organize your videos and make it easier for your audience to find the first video or the newest video. It allows them to start at a well marked point in the season and continue watching from that point.

5. Call-to-Action to Others – One part of marketing is doing a call-to-action (CTA). These are the buttons or wordings asking others to "click here" or "sign up." It is your attempt to convince someone to do something, to nudge them to take action. Make sure that after your video is done that your audience knows what they can do to support your series. By using captions and annotations during or near the end of the video you can give the viewer messages directly asking them to rate, comment, or share your video. But don't overuse this feature. Try not to distract from the story and don't ask too many things at once.

6. Your Call-to-Action to Share – Make sure to share that video widely in all of your social media networks in those first 24 hours of its release. Use the embed code to embed it on blog posts and on your website.

7. YouTube Partner Program – Once you reach a certain level of traffic you can apply to become a YouTube Partner. The partnership comes with advertisements, paid subscriptions, and merchandise opportunities in addition to other resources. More than a million creators from over 30 countries belong to the partnership program.

8. To MCN or Not to MCN – At some point if you become big enough you may be asked to join an MCN (Multi-Channel Network) or you may request to join one. I'll talk more about them in the Distribution chapter coming up.

9. Review the Stats – YouTube has one of the best analytics features from the major video distribution platforms, so make good use of it for adjustments in your marketing plans. You can see where viewers are being referred from and you should use that information to customize what websites you reach out to and make sure you are paying extra attention to your primary referrers. Also see if certain sites are linking to certain videos. You may also want to fine-tune which sites you reach out to with particular videos, in case one series of videos is more popular than another.

Instagram

Released October 2010, Instagram is an online photo sharing, video sharing and social networking service that provides users the ability to take pictures and videos (up to 15 seconds), then apply a digital filter to them and share them via social media networks. In March 2014, Instagram announced that they have 200 million users with 60 million photos shared daily. So there is no doubt it is worth paying attention to, especially if you are aiming for mobile device users and young demographics which are the core group that use this network. Of course, your core audience may not be strongly using Instagram, so be sure to double check that first before you put too much energy into this tool.

But how do you use it? First, create your account. Similar rules as the other social networks: add a profile picture (should represent you or your series), write a bio (in 200 words or less), and connect to a website (that is mobile friendly).

Instagram is all about images, so promote your series through images: behind-the-scenes pictures of production, images with quotes, creative plays on a popular meme, and pictures that let the personalities of those in the crew and cast shine through. You could also run contests challenging viewers to dress like their favorite character, add comedic subtitles to a still shot, or some other fun contest that is interactive and tied to the brand of your series somehow. And don't forget, share those Instagram pictures on all of your social media networks including tricks like hashtags and a call-to-action asking for likes, comments, or something else.

Pinterest

Pinterest, which first had a small launch in March 2010 and after going with a larger release grew quickly, calls itself a visual discovery tool that allows users to upload, save, sort and manage images (called pins) and other content like videos through collections called pinboards. A strong contender for something to try in marketing if you have the images to use. It tends to skew more female and I would suggest checking the related topics of your series to see first if there is a substantial following on this network before trying it.

Flickr

Flickr is an image-hosting and video-hosting service created in 2004. This online community can be used to share and embed photographs. It is very popular with photographers. I would suggest if you use this one to join groups that have interests connected somehow to your series. For example, the web series *Parings,* where food is an important prop used in the episodes, could join a group about taking pictures of food. But, if you share photos be sure they are high-quality photos, since so many professional photographers use the site; otherwise you might not leave the impression you are hoping for.

Tumblr

Tumblr is a microblogging social networking website. It allows users to post multimedia and other content to a short-form blog. Users can follow other user blogs. On March 3, 2014, it was announced by Tumblr that it hosts over 174.2 million blogs. It has mixed results with web series marketing. There is no doubt that image sharing on Tumblr is usually the most successful type of post. If your web series has a lot of images to share, it might be worth trying this social media network.

Social News Sites

There are a number of social news sites out there than can give your videos or press an increase in traffic. Social news sites take news submitted by users and ranks them according to popularity. Each one has their own approach on how content is sorted and each one has its own type of audiences with different interests. Some examples include Digg, Reddit, Mixx, Fark, MetaFilter, Newsvine and Sphinn. Those sites are mostly general news sites. If you want help seeking out more or finding ones that work well for your project, you can do a Google search using some combination of social news site and the keywords that fit your project.

You'll want to fine tune your news submissions to the kind of headlines and stories that seem to do well on that news site to better improve your chances of getting the news ranked high. Don't just cookie cutter your news the exact same way in all of your social news site submissions.

StumbleUpon

StumbleUpon is a sort of search engine, but more accurately called a discovery engine. It finds and recommends web content to users and allows them to rate websites, photos, and videos that are personalized to their interests. In 2006 the StumbleUpon Video section was aggregating bookmarked videos and shuffling them so users can view different videos one at a time and vote for them. It can support a wide range of videos from YouTube, Google Video, Vimeo, Dailymotion, and many more. You can submit videos by signing up for an account and installing a browser toolbar. Once submitting you can ask your social media connections to "stumble" your video.

TV.com – A sort of online TV guide powered by social media. It has listings of TV shows, movies, and web series. It allows you to follow your favorite shows, join fan communities, share news, etc. You can join the site and submit new shows (like your web series) by emailing: newshows@tv.com

IMDb

The Internet Movie Database is where you can find information on nearly every movie and TV series out there, including their cast and crew. So you better be there too. It is a sure thing that someone in the biz will look you up at some point if they want to see what kind of projects you've worked on. Although there are forums on IMDb, this platform is more about just making it easier for people to find you online and hopefully your project. The site doesn't have a web series category, but they can often fall under "TV series."

You can try adding your project yourself, but until you've built up some kind of history on IMDb it is hard to get your things on the system. A surefire way of doing it is submitting to a qualifying festival via Withoutabox. So be sure you are in the database and make sure your information is kept up-to-date. It is the next best thing to a résumé.

You may want to consider upgrading to IMDb Pro which allows you to better customize your IMDb page and opens up to tools to aid in casting. So if you need to do casting or you are an actor, then the upgrade will likely be worth it to you.

Wiki

A wiki is a Content Management System that allows people to add, modify, or delete content in collaboration with other users. There are many fan wikis online for different TV shows or books where fans collect information about the series. You could create such a wiki for fans to use if that might fit your overall marketing plan or make sense with the type of show you are doing.

One of the most famous wikis (beside WikiLeaks) is Wikipedia. It is a sort of online community-driven encyclopedia. Once your series is online and had some successes, you can submit to Wikipedia. But Wikipedia can be pretty picky, so you have to make sure to have external news links and that you feel the series has reached a level of popularity to allow it to be accepted. Otherwise, be prepared for the possibility that it might be removed from admins.

Email Marketing

Marketing with email may seem old fashioned and intrusive, but it is actually one of the best ways to market. If someone signs up for an email list, then you know they are interested and you are just keeping them updated on news for the project they are interested in. As long as you don't abuse that email list by spamming their email box, then you have perhaps one of the most powerful marketing tools at hand. The use of third-party email providers lets you create enewsletters for free or inexpensively and can be integrated with most social media networks.

First off you need a third-party email provider which will allow you to design professional looking newsletters that can be sent in bulk to a list and allow you to track them. One of the most popular is Mail Chimp (http://mailchimp.com) which is free currently at under 2,000 subscribers and is one of the more user-friendly ones out there. But it isn't the only option; some other popular ones include Campaign Monitor (http://www.campaignmonitor.com), Constant Contact (http://www.constantcontact.com), and Vertical Response (http://www.verticalresponse.com).

But setting up that account is useless unless you get people to actually join the list. You need to add an opt-in subscription email box to your website, blog, Facebook Page, and anywhere you can. Make sure to spread the word ... I know, I know, it is marketing your marketing, but a necessary evil. At events online and offline ask people to join the list. Use your social media networks to point people to where they can subscribe. Then make sure to schedule when the newsletters will be sent out and stick to that schedule, only breaking it for big news to share. This way those on the list learn when to expect updates and know they won't be spammed.

I would also suggest, if the account will allow you to, to send those that unsubscribe an auto-message for feedback. Not only might they change their mind, but at the very least you'll learn if you have done something wrong that may be upsetting others on the list.

Hire a Publicist or PMD?

Remember, if marketing is not your specialty and you need help, you can hire a publicist to provide advice or help you manage a marketing campaign at key moments. A new crew role that is becoming more and more common is the Producer of Marketing and Distribution (PMD). The PMD is typically responsible for developing the marketing strategy and execution. They create marketing content like behind-the-scenes footage, interviews, photography, and more. And they manage all of the social media accounts. They could also manage other publicity, events, reach out to influencers, and more. It is a very new kind of job position, but is becoming quickly more and more popular with its growing effectiveness.

Online Advertising

Don't forget, you can pay for advertising. I've touched on some of that, but many of the major social media networks I've discussed have options for paid ads of some sort. It can be a useful boost, if you have the funds. It helps build awareness, drive geo-specific niche audiences to your series, can drive traffic to your website, and hopefully give you a surge of views in the early stages of the season. Just explore what options there are for the social media networks you choose. Also, don't forget that you can place ads on niche web-sites that appeal to your audience.

Premiere Party

Everyone loves to party and if you can afford it, setting up a pre-miere party for the first or first few episodes can be a great way to generate excitement for the premiere and reward the cast and crew with a fun time. Plus ... you get tons of pictures to share on Twitter, Facebook, etc. Marketing never stops and these kind of events can add some fun to the workload.

Festivals

You want to submit to select festivals to pick up some laurels and awards to help earn a little more respect and generate some more buzzworthy news. You can also make great contacts, but we'll talk more about that in an upcoming chapter.

Transmedia Producing

Transmedia Producing or Transmedia Storytelling is developing a story across multiple media and often with a degree of audience interaction or collaboration. In older multi-medium strategies for a franchise, there might be novels that take place in the same setting but don't really affect the TV show or vice versa. But with a trans-media approach certain elements in each medium would affect each other. Ideally a viewer or reader will enjoy each element by itself, but have greater appreciation of the overall storyworld if they read or view all of the various pieces in the transmedia puzzle. It is a really exciting field of producing which has grown so much over the years that in 2010 the Producers Guild of America (PGA) voted on and ratified a new credit, the Transmedia Producer.

Speaking of the PGA, why don't I just quote their official description of the credit.

"A Transmedia Narrative project or franchise must consist of three (or more) narrative storylines existing within the same fictional universe on any of the following platforms: Film, Television, Short Film, Broadband, Publishing, Comics, Animation, Mobile, Special Venues, DVD/Blu-ray/CD-ROM, Narrative Commercial and Marketing rollouts, and other technologies that may or may not currently exist. These narrative extensions are NOT the same as re-purposing material from one platform to be cut or re-purposed to different platforms."

Lost, Matrix, SyFy's *Defiance* are a few examples of traditional franchises that experimented with transmedia. *Lost's* expanded universe included tie-in novels; *Lost: Missing Pieces* (13 two-to-five minute mobisodes (short episodes made for mobile devices); *Lost: Via Domus* video game; diegetic artifacts (the book *Bad Twin*); web sites for fictional elements in the story; and other alternate reality extensions like the five-month interactive marketing campaign called *The Lost Experience.* For example, *Bad Twin* was a book seen in the episode "Two for the Road." Sawyer is reading a manuscript called *Bad Twin,* which Jack throws into a fire during a confrontation. The fictional author of the book was supposed to have been on board Oceanic 815 and died in the crash. After that episode the book was released in bookstores, offering fans the chance to read the ending that Sawyer didn't get to read. A fun way to take an item in a story and bring it into the real world. There is no reason why you can't do something similar.

Web series episodes, feature films, short films, video games, tabletop games, comic books, webcomics, novels, online fiction, character in-story social media accounts (Twitter, Facebook, etc.), QR codes, in-story web sites, etc. There are so many options that you can layer together to make the storyworld greater than just one platform. An Alternate Reality Game (ARG) might be used to link the different pieces, especially if you want more interaction with the fans.

So when you design your series, think about ways to explore that storyworld in more than one medium. Some web series have experimented with Transmedia storytelling; just watch that the time spent and the money used doesn't take too much away from your series.

ATTENTION! ATTENTION!

There you go, a crash course on marketing for web series. As you can tell it is a lot of work, but it can make a huge difference on how successful your series will be. So don't be shy, start spreading the word. Make a marketing schedule and let everyone know about your new web series that they shouldn't miss. Remember, this is the only way your series can be heard in the crowd of web series voices. It could be the greatest series ever, but if no one hears about it, it will just be the greatest series with no one watching it.

Suggested Reading

Transmedia producing and online marketing in general are important aspects of a successful career in creating and promoting your web series. Unless you want to pay an expert to take over, you should explore every avenue for increasing your knowledge and abilities in this increasingly essential role. I recommend *Make Your Story Really Stink Big* by Houston Howard for further research.

CHAPTER 6

THE MANY PATHS
OF DISTRIBUTION

So you got your web series created and you are spreading the word, but how are you going to share your great series? Luckily, this part of a web series is the easy part. Distributing online is a breeze. The tricky part is picking the best options that make sense for your series.

Before I talk about online distribution, keep in mind other forms of distribution are always possible. During the life of a series or movie you have various windows of distribution. A window of distribution is the period of time your film or series is available for a particular form of media.

Here are a few options:

- Theatrical Release
- DIY Theatrical (Four Walling)
- Pay Television
- DVD/Blu-Ray
- Network Television
- Cable television
- Closed circuit (hotels, buses, airplanes, cruise ships)
- Online Distribution

Monetize This!

By far the most difficult thing to do in a web series is make money. There is more potential to make money than a short film, but not on the same levels of profit that a good feature film could produce.

1. Ad Revenue Model

One of the easiest models to do, with often just a click needed, is to put ads on your videos by a video platform like YouTube or Blip. The amount you make is based on CPM (cost per thousand) and can vary widely depending on the distributor and the niche your series is in. But be aware you will need to get tens of thousands of views on each video to make any kind of money. Just be careful you don't pour on so many ads (sometimes you have options for pre-roll, mid-roll, post-roll, etc.) that you frustrate new viewers and risk a slow growth in your audience.

This model is where non-scripted or sketch comedy tends to excel because you can create videos quickly and cheaply. The constant quick turnaround enables you to keep viewers coming back and the low overhead means the return doesn't have to be high. This typically works best on YouTube or similar ad models.

2. Subscription Model

If you use Netflix, then you know how subscription models work. The web series will get either a percent of profits from the subscribers or will be paid a flat rate for the rights to add the series for a limited time. Although not as easy to get into, this model can usually provide you higher revenue. You'll need to make sure to keep your production quality high and perhaps make a few connections to manage to get your series on a subscription model.

3. Sponsors or Branded Model

Sponsored series were huge for a couple of years, but they are much more difficult to arrange now. But some examples include: *Easy to Assemble* (IKEA), *Leap Year* (Hiscox), *The Temp Life* (Spherion), *Dating Rules from My Future Self* (Schick's Quattro and Ford Escape), *Always Open* (Denny's), *The Return of D Rose* (Adidas Basketball), and *Falling For You* (Target). This can be a great model for making money for your series, if you can manage to arrange it. The only potential drawback is if the brand takes on too much creative control hurting the series, but so far brands have tended to give a lot of freedom to creators.

4. Crowdfunding Model

I've already spoken extensively in the funding chapter on how to use crowdfunding. That is a "raise the funds before you film" model, unless you do one of the newer subscriber types of crowdfunding platforms. With that option you are essentially doing the subscription model. A growing in popularity option for web series creators who become frustrated with low returns from some of the other models.

5. Merchandise model

Not really a monetization strategy that works best by itself. It usually works better when paired up with one of the above models. This is selling shirts, glasses, posters, ebooks, and other items that may have logos or images from the series. You could also sell unique items that are used as props in the series. If you gain a large fanbase it could be nice supplemental income, but not something to rely on by itself.

6. Licensing

It is possible you will be approached by a company to license rights to air your series on some medium other than the web. For example, we were approached to air *Reality on Demand* on public buses in Mexico. There are no rules on these kind of deals though, so you may do it for nothing but exposure or they may offer a decent amount. Just be careful what you sign and make sure you don't give them rights to license the video for an unlimited amount of time. After all, if you manage to license a deal with a larger company like Syfy or BET, you'll want a way out because they may not want to share air time with anyone else.

Which Distributor?

Let's focus on the online distribution, probably a large part of why you are reading this book. With online distribution being so new, I've heard conflicting breakdowns on terminology on different distribution platforms: VoD, On-Demand Television, Movies-on-Demand, On-Demand Programming, VOD on the Web, VOD on Cable, Internet-on-Demand Video, IP-based Video, IPTV Broadcasting, Internet HDTV, Internet Video, Web Video, Video Webcasting, Webcasting, Pay-As-You-Go, Live-Streaming Video and On-Demand Streaming Video, Broadcast Internet, Switched Digital Video, Video Dial Tone, Application on Demand, Entertainment on Demand, On-Demand Services, Television On-Demand, etc. Sometimes I feel like people are just making up stuff in an attempt to seem different. There are a lot of terms bantered about, but I'm going to keep it simple. I separate your online distribution options into three broad categories:

❶ **Transactional:** This is where you pay an amount to download or stream a video.

❷ **Subscription:** This is where you subscribe to a distribution platform paying a recurring fee to have access to a collection of films/series.

❸ **Ad Sponsored or Free:** These are videos that you download or stream for free with either no advertising or with advertising included.

Since some of the larger online distribution platforms are trying to offer more than one option I won't separate them by category, but will instead list them and tell you which kinds of distribution they offer and some other basic information you'll need to know.

YouTube (http://youtube.com)

I've already spoken about how popular YouTube is online. It is the most compatible embedded video player currently out, is the second most popular search engine, and has lots of extra features for enhancing your videos. In the old days it was limited by how many minutes you could upload or standard definition only, but now it can be 1080p, allows you to upload feature length films, and includes monetization options. It is also easy to use and more transparent in your analytics data than many other video distributors.

The downside is that because they are so large you can't speak to a live person, so if there is a problem it will be hard to get it fixed. YouTube is also very sensitive about copyrights, and there's nothing wrong with that. But sometimes they will block a video or take away ads without warning and can be tough to fix. Also, although YouTube is hugely popular there are countless channels so it can be tough to stand out on the platform on your own starting out.

Independent YouTube Multi-Channel Networks

If you want to use YouTube, but are afraid of getting lost in the noise, you can join a Multi-Channel Network (MCN), organizations that work with YouTube channels to offer help with product, programming, funding, cross-promotion, partner management, digital rights management, monetization/sales, and/or audience development, all for a percentage of the AdSense revenue. Examples of MCNs are: Machinima, Big Frame, Maker Studios, Fullscreen, etc. In 2014 larger, more traditional studios started buying MCNs. Maker Studios was reportedly sold to Disney for $500 million and Big Frame sold to Dreamworks through AwesomenessTV for $15 million. Will this tread continue and what it means for web series creators remains to be seen.

There has been controversy with MCNs, which I talked about in the earlier history section of the book, such as talk of unfair contracts. So be careful what you sign and be sure it makes sense for your long-term plans.

Vimeo (http://vimeo.com)

Founded in November 2004, this video platform has always been respected for quality video image and is popular with filmmakers. It was actually the first online video platform to permit HD at 720p. Vimeo has developed its own community with what they call Vimeans being active members in the community. There are also annual Vimeo awards.

You can upload videos for free, but there are pay accounts (Basic, Plus, Pro) that allow you to upload larger video files, have fast upload times, advanced analytics, etc. There never used to be a way to make money off your videos though in Vimeo, until 2013 when it rolled out tip-jar and pay-to-view options. Web series creators are still experimenting with these features and how well those options are generating income for creators.

Blip (http://blip.tv)

Founded in 2005, Blip has been one of the top non-YouTube choices for web series creators. Money for creators is made by shared ad revenue profits. In 2013, Blip was bought by Maker Studios, which came with new requirements that uploaded video had to be a web series and reach a certain standard of quality.

JTS (Just The Story) (http://jts.tv)

Just The Story (at JTS.tv) is a video distributor with the mantra of "No Ads, Just The Story." It is a sort of Netflix for high-quality, independently produced web series. For $3.99 per month, a subscriber gains access to all shows on JTS and half of all subscription revenue received goes directly to the web series creators. I've heard nothing but good things about them from other web series creators. So if you are interested in offering your series on a subscription platform then this might be a great option for you. It is much smaller than Netflix, but that smaller company comes with benefits in communication with the company and it seems they have a fair share of revenue.

Dailymotion (http://www.dailymotion.com)

This very large video platform is a based in France. It is huge in Europe especially. I haven't seen many US-based series launch their series exclusively to this platform The horror series *Camera Obscura* being one of the only exceptions I can think of, which premiered on Dailymotion and spread from there. You can earn up to 70% from ad revenue.

Amazon — Createspace (https://www.createspace.com)

Createspace, which is owned by Amazon, provides some interesting options for both creating DVDs or video downloads on Amazon Instant Video. You can offer your videos on Amazon Instant Video as either Download to Own or Download to Rent. Amazon pays you royalties from purchases.

Hulu & Hulu Plus (http://hulu.com)

Hulu is one of the most popular videos platforms online for scripted content and has an extensive library of television shows and movies trying to compete with Netflix. Hulu is ad supported and Hulu Plus is a subscription service. Hulu can be profitable for web series, but like Netflix it is not easy to be accepted to and you will almost have to get a distributor to arrange the deal or team-up with other content creators.

iTunes (https://www.apple.com/itunes)

To get greater exposure for your series you can add your show on Apple's iTunes as a free download. You won't make money, but you can add subscribers and access a large potential audience.

Netflix (https://www.netflix.com)

Founded in 1997, this is by far the biggest subscription video distributor currently out there. As of January 2014 it had 44 million subscribers. Of course, with a monster that size it has both good and bad sides to it. First, if you are by yourself it will be very hard for you to get your web series added. You would need to get a distributor to arrange the deal or team-up with other content creators.

Distrify (https://distrify.com)

This interesting digital suite allows you to upload and post your trailer on websites, social media, etc., and when people click on the player they are given options to download or stream the video. They could also be given options to buy a DVD, Blu-ray, merchandise, or share the trailer (with the built-in options to see the actual film or series) on all major social media platforms. There are various monthly plans, starting with the free Indie plan that allows you to sell rentals to other plans that cost per month, but provide new options like download-to-own, selling merchandise, branded VOD player, etc.

VHX (http://www.vhx.tv)

VHX is very new with its leaving the beta phase and being open to everyone in 2014. It offers some very interesting opportunities for web series creators and filmmakers in general. And tries to create a non-exclusive platform that offers social media integration, SEO optimization, analytics tools, and monetization. The platform provides streaming and DRM-free downloads of video content. Well worth checking out to see if it might work for your series or other film projects you may have.

Other Video Aggregators

There are a number of video distribution platforms that are fairly easy to submit your series to. Some have no monetization option and others provide a percentage of revenue. Here are a few.

- **MyTeeVee** — http://myteevee.tv
- **Metacafe** — http://www.metacafe.com/
- **Nutral TV** — http://nutraltv.com
- **Van Indie Films Channel** — http://vanindiefilms.com
- **VBCtv** — http://www.vbctv.com
- **Veoh** — http://www.veoh.com
- **Vidwala** — http://vidwala.com
- **Web Series Channe**l — http://www.webserieschannel.com/

Torrents (the legal kind)

If you are looking for more exposure and not worried about turning a profit off the video itself, you could also offer your series on a bittorrent site. I know, surprise, they aren't all illegal downloads. But since so many are ripe with pirated copies I won't list them here, but just do a search online if you want to go that path.

Live Streaming

If you want to do a live show perhaps where you talk to camera or have guests, then you can use various live streaming services for that. The most popular being Ustream, Livestream, and Sickam. These type of services usually allow you to record the shows and archive them for a channel.

Offline Distribution

Don't forget about offline distribution, like selling DVDs and Blu-rays. But beware; the further you stray from online distribution the most likely your project starts morphing into one of the more traditional mediums, which can affect the type of contracts you've signed with SAG-AFTRA or others.

CHAPTER 7

AWARDS, PLEASE?

"Every festival has its own kind of flavor." — Adam J. Cohen,
Founder of the Unofficial Google+ Film Festival

E very filmmaker knows that film festivals play a crucial role in getting attention for their film. The old approach was to hit Sundance or a few other crucial festivals, create some buzz, then a distributor picks the film up. Done and done. Of course, only a minority found success and nowadays even less can make this work.

When I did my first web series I thought, "Finally, no more film festival circuit where I spend tons of money for my film to possibly be seen ... I just go straight to the audience." I realized quickly that film festivals still have a big place in helping my series get attention. It's not even so much about having people sit down and see, but more about the attention that can be given for it being accepted or nominated and winning. Those laurels help your project gain attention and reach new audiences. I wouldn't advise you spending a ton of money on film festivals (which is easy to do with the quick growth of them accepting web series), but strategically pick those that your type of show is likely to appeal to. That will require research ... I heard that groan, but it is a necessary evil. You have to see what kind of shows have done well. They may lean toward low-budget or they may lean toward high budget productions. They may heavily favor series that have web celebs or lean towards a particular genre. They may love science fiction/ fantasy, or those genres may get no traction.

This echoes what Adam J. Cohen, found of the Unofficial Google+ Film Festival told me. He said, "Every festival has its own kind of flavor." And that is very true. So learn what flavors these festivals have, and primarily submit to the ones that lean toward your type of project.

All artists wants validation from their peers. Awards not only fulfill that need, but also serve as great marketing tools. There are a growing number of awards that are available for web series creators and a quickly growing number of film festivals either made just for web television or ones that are including the web series category where it was once ignored.

But what is out there and which ones are worth your money? First I'll talk about a good way to find film festivals. Then I'll break down the major awards and take a look at the quickly growing number of web series festivals.

Withoutabox

https://www.withoutabox.com/
An excellent resource to find festivals and submit to them is Withoutabox. The website was founded in January 2000 to help independent filmmakers self-distribute their films. In January 2008, Withoutabox was acquired by IMDb (a division of Amazon.com).

Withoutabox allows filmmakers to search over 5,000 film festivals across six continents and submit their films to well-known festivals like Sundance and the Toronto International Film Festival. The service allows you to upload your project so festivals can request submissions via the web which helps save you money from the usual DVDs via mail screening process for festivals. The ownership by Amazon also allows Withoutabox users to create IMDb pages for their projects and self-distribute (DVD, VOD, and streaming video) via Amazon's CreateSpace.

Unfortunately, at the time of this writing, Withoutabox still doesn't provide an easy way to search for festivals that accept web series. But fear not, I've collected a large list of festivals and award shows you can consider.

But, before I go over this list I've compiled, I do want to give you a few websites you can also search for other festivals that may or not be web series friendly.

- BestInFest (listing around 1,700 festivals) http://www.bestin-fest.com/festivallist.html

- FilmFestivals.com at (surprise) http://www.filmfestivals.com/

- Festival Focus http://www.festivalfocus.org/

Festival & Award Show List

Now on to my list of festivals and award shows which I've broken down into three categories:

- Web Series Festivals & Awards

- Other Film Festivals & Awards

- Conventions

Web Series–Friendly Film Festivals

The concept of a festival focused on just web series has been quickly growing in the last few years. Web series festivals and awards are made specifically for web programs. They are younger than other festivals. The first exclusively web television award show was the Streamy Awards which started in 2009. LA Webfest was the first web series festival starting in 2010. So quality of these festivals and their life span may vary, but they have quickly grown. They started really exploding onto the scene in 2013 and 2014 with a huge jump in the number of them mostly in North America and Europe. I've listed the most established ones first, then the rest of the newer festivals in alphabetical order.

Next up are more traditional film festivals and award shows that have been around longer and started with their focus on traditional television or films, but in recent years have made it possible for web series to submit. Their attention to web series can vary, but they are more established and respected by a larger pool of professionals and critics.

Last, we have conventions. These tend to favor certain genres, primarily from the comic book, gaming, sci-fi, or fantasy flavors. The conventions, with booths, panels, contests, etc., tend to get more attention, but within them are film festivals that web series can enter and opportunities to get on some of those panels, too.

Speaking of booths, don't spend too much money on this type of marketing. Thomas Gofton, creator of the web series *Mind's Eye,* advised me that if he had to do it again he would have stuck with smaller cons and festivals only for his first season. He spent a small fortune on booths and festivals, and learned quickly that at larger cons he had wasted his money because the more well-known (and higher budget) traditional productions were getting all of the attention. So if you decide to do booths, stick to a grassroots movement of smaller cons and festivals to get the most out of your money and time.

Web Series Festivals & Awards

IAWTV Awards

http://www.hollywebfestival.com/
This is considered one of the top awards that specialize in web series. As you may remember in the history overview earlier in the book, the International Academy of Web Television once handed out the Streamy Awards, but after breaking away from the profit group that ran that award show, the IAWTV created their own award show. Originally, members of the IAWTV would vote in each category for all submissions, which could sometimes be over 100 web series. Yuck! Not only was it tough for members to wade through it all, but it lead to criticism that only those shows already well known either through publicity or through connections in LA or NY (where the majority of members lived) had any real chance of being nominated, much less winning.

To help with this, starting in 2014 the board decided that judges would be selected and they would screen categories that had no entries they had ties to. The judges picked five nominees for each category and then the members voted for the winners. I was flattered to be asked to be one of those judges. I had a week to watch over 100 entries, but it was an amazing responsibility and I loved it. Although not everything I felt should have gotten nominated did, there is no doubt that every nominee was strong. So don't worry if you aren't in a major IAWTV city; your chances are better than ever and even getting nominated is something to brag about.

You don't have to be a member of the IAWTV to submit your series, but joining not only gets you discounts to these awards but also to a few other major web series festivals. You also benefit from networking online with other members.

Streamys

http://www.streamys.org/about/streamys/

The very first web series–specific award show was the Streamy Awards. On March 28, 2009, with the combined efforts of the IAWTV and the website Tubefilter, the Streamy Awards premiered online. After the 2nd Annual Streamy Awards, the IAWTV split off and made their own award show.

The Streamy awards took some time off to regroup and returned big on February 17th, 2013. Tubefilter teamed up with Dick Clark Productions to host the 3rd Annual Streamy Awards at the Hollywood Palladium in Los Angeles. With live music guests and celebrity guests, plus a high production value, the show was considered an improvement over the 2nd Annual Streamy Awards show. As of the time of this writing there has been no news of a 2014 Streamy Awards show. This could mean the award show is done or taking another break. Keep an eye on their website for a possible new award show and be careful with your budget because this particular award has historically been one of the more expensive ones.

LA Webfest

http://www.lawebfest.com/

The Los Angeles Web Series Festival (LA Webfest) is the oldest web series festival in the world. It was founded in 2010 by Emmy-winning producer Michael Ajakwe, Jr., for the purpose of screening web series and allowing web series creators to meet. The festival selects a wide range of web series of different genres from all over the world. In 2013, the festival screened 262 series. They truly have lived up to their goal of being international over the years by screening series from 19 different countries.

Due to the large number of selections, this festival is a good one to submit to for a chance to get selected, no matter what country you are from. They also have panels with different web series creators giving advice which could be helpful, especially if you are new to the industry.

Indie Series Awards

http://www.indieseriesawards.com/

Founded by the We Love Soaps editorial team in 2009, the Indie Series Awards was created to (in their words) "...celebrate the best in independently produced, scripted entertainment created for the Web." Until 2014, the awards were actually called the Indie Soap Awards, but as you can imagine, that caused some confusion on what kind of genres of web series could be submitted.

"Daytime soaps are making a huge comeback in the ratings but the term "soap" has always been used in a negative way by the mainstream media," founder Roger Newcomb told me. "If a movie is bad, it's called a soap by the reviewer. We love many, many primetime series and web series that do not consider themselves soaps. They are serials. For the awards show, changing the name from Soap to Series was the best thing I could do to help bring added attention to the best indie web series. From press to potential sponsors, that word makes a big positive difference, despite my personal love for soaps."

The ISA is more of an award show than a festival, although they do play a lot of clips during the awards ceremony. They have an official Pre-Party the night before the ceremony for networking opportunities and fun. The main event is the red carpet and awards ceremony, followed by the official After Party. Also, a few web series producers organize a web series panel discussion each year.

One of the unique things the ISA does is try to focus only on independently produced web series and do not mix in studio-produced series. For the 5th Annual Indie Series Awards there were 56 nominated series.

HollyWeb Festival

http://www.hollywebfestival.com/

Another web festival I've heard many positive things about is the HollyWeb Festival. I think you can guess by the name where it takes place. Yup, you guessed it: Hollywood, Alabama. OK, just kidding. This is another web series festival in Los Angeles and I've heard great things about it from web series creators who have attended.

Screenings are at Raleigh Studios in the state-of-the-art Chaplin Theater. You would be hard-pressed to find many screening venues for web series that can outdo it. The awards ceremony is at the historic Avalon Hollywood with the traditional red carpet walk being replaced with a blue carpet.

The festival has categories for short- and long-form (depending if episodes exceed 10 minutes), and only two episodes must be completed to be considered as a series. The festival welcomes international series and documentaries.

Atlanta Web Fest

http://atlwebfest.com/

The first Atlanta Web Fest was in 2013 at Georgia Tech in Atlanta. The festival includes screenings, panels, and workshops. To submit, you must have at least three episodes in the series, preferably under 10 minutes each.

Austin Web Fest

http://www.austinwebfestival.com

The Austin Web Fest is billed as the first web series festival in Texas. This festival is still new and taking submissions for the first time in 2014, so there isn't much information on it yet.

Baja Web Fest

http://bajawebfest.com/

The first web series festival in Mexico. This festival is also very new and taking submissions for the first time in 2014.

Campi Flegrei Web Series Fest

www.campiflegreiwebseriesfest.it

Held in Naples, Italy, this web series festival started in 2013. It looks for homegrown web series, but also accepts them from any country. For their first year, submissions were free of charge.

Carballo Interplay

http://carballointerplay.com/

The first web series festival in Spain which hit the scene with their first event in Spain on April 2014 in the little town of Galicia.

Celebrate the Web

http://www.celebratetheweb.com

Celebrate the Web was started by Jenni Powell and Kim Evey (producer of *The Guild*). It came about [after the controversy with the second Streamy Awards], said Powell. "I was writing for Tubefilter at the time and was in a very difficult position of being the journalist that had to cover the Streamy Awards for Tubefilter, because the guys who run Tubefilter also put on the Streamy Awards." After asking the web series community what they would have liked differently with the Streamy Awards, they came up with this event. It has morphed over the years, but is primarily a web series pilot contest that allows seven days for creators to make their pilot; a web series spin on the 48-hour film contest format.

DC Web Fest

http://dcwebfest.co

This web series festival in Washington, DC, was started in 2013 and for their second year they added new categories like blogging, gaming, robotics, and digital media applications.

FEW – Web Fest

http://www.few-webfest.com

FEW (Spanish Webseries Festival) is a new web series festival out of Madrid with an inaugural year in 2014.

IMMaginario WebFest

http://www.immaginario.tv/immwebfest/
This web series festival based in Perugia, Italy, started in 2013 with a large selection of Italian web series, around 100 shows.

Liege Web Fest

http://liegewebfest.be/
Based out of Liege, Belgium, this web series festival is held by the Fédération Wallonie-Bruxelles and tends to highlight projects which have been awarded by partner festivals.

Marseille Web Fest

http://www.marseillewebfest.org
Marseille Web Fest is the first European festival, founded in 2011 by president Jean-Michel Albert. The selected international web series from those submitted are chosen by a jury of professionals from around the world. Besides the screenings and awards, there are also meet-ups and panels.

Melbourne Web Fest

http://melbournewebfest.com
Melbourne Web Fest is the first and currently only festival dedicated exclusively to web series in Australia. Its first festival was in 2013 with screenings and included panels on Transmedia Storytelling & Economics of Digital Media. The festival recognizes various genres including fantasy/sci-fi, drama, comedy, nonfiction, and suspense. It also has a Grand Jury Prize and the first year's prize went to a German sci-fi series called *Mission Backup Earth*.

Miami Web Fest

http://miamiwebfest.com/
The Miami Web Series Festival, featuring screenings, speakers, workshops, and panel discussions, is the first of its kind in Miami, Florida. The team behind it have designed it with the hope to give web series creators, executives, and sponsors a forum for "interaction and discovery." Most of the awards are broken into best series awards separated by genre. One noteworthy award category is the Diversity Award.

New York City Webfest

http://nycwebfest.com/
This new web series festival will premiere in 2014 and is billed as the first international web series festival to take place in New York.

Raindance London Web Fest

http://raindancefestival.org/webfest-2014/
The first Raindance London Web Fest took place on September 2013. There were 50 international web series screened, including the world premieres of *Producing Juliet* and *Lab Rats*. Besides screenings there are also panels with web series creators and experts. The festival features fiction and nonfiction projects and submissions must have at least three episodes in English or with subtitles to be considered.

Roma Web Fest

http://www.romawebfest.it/
The first Roma Web Fest took place in Rome on 27, 28, and 29 of September, 2013. It bills itself as the first official Italian festival for web series. Its goal is connecting Italian and international web series producers with the Italian television and film industries.

Rome Web Awards

http://www.romewebawards.it
Another festival in Rome that starts in 2014. It includes not just web series, but also short films. It is a very new festival and there isn't much information on it yet.

Singapore Web Fest (formerly HK Web Fest)

http://www.webfest.hk/
This festival's goal is to promote and celebrate transmedia, branded entertainment, and web series with an objective of creating communication between the East and the West. The first year of the festival was in 2013 in Hong Kong, but for 2014 the organization moved the festival to Singapore. The first year featured more "microfilms" than web series. The first year also had several panel discussions and hangouts in English and Cantonese.

TO WebFest (Toronto Web Series Festival)

http://www.towebfest.com

This Canadian web series festival held in Toronto is an initiative promoted by the IWCC (Independent Webseries Creators of Canada) which is a non-profit organization. The inaugural year for the festival was 2014 and it has screenings, panel discussions, live events, and signings.

Vancouver Web Fest

http://www.vancouverwebfest.com/index.html

Billed as "Canada's Premiere International Web Series Festival," this festival's inaugural year was 2014. Although there is a focus on Canadian productions, entries can come from anywhere in the world but must be in English or subtitled. The first year had selections from the United States, Canada, UK, France, Australia, Ireland, Columbia, Mexico, and other countries. Similar to other award shows or festivals, the series must have at least three episodes to be considered. Their award categories for "Best" are diverse: Comedy, Drama, Action/Adventure, Fantasy/Science Fiction, Reality, Documentary/ Non-Fiction, Animation, Mystery/Thriller, Horror, Musical, Foreign, App Based Series, Overall Series, Actor, and Actress.

Other Film Festivals & Awards

Action on Film Fest

http://www.aoffest.com/submit-your-work.asp

Founded in 2004, the Action on Film Fest is an international film festival currently held in Monrovia, California. The festival has been held in other cities previously. Despite the name, the festival does accept all major genres and is not limited to just action films. They accept submissions for Features, Shorts, Experimental, Animation, Music Videos, Action Sequences, etc. The festival includes a film market and there are prizes.

Bushwick Film Festival

http://bushwickfilmfestival.com/

Founded in 2007, the Bushwick Film Festival is a project sponsored by Fractured Atlas, a non-profit arts service organization. The festival strives to provide a unique platform for independent filmmakers and new media artists to share their stories and engage with a diverse community of film lovers and industry professionals. The festival accepts submissions for web series, short films, and feature documentaries.

British Academy Television Awards

http://www.bafta.org/television/awards and http://www.bafta.org/television/craft-awards/

Founded in 1947, the British Academy of Film and Television Arts (BAFTA) supports, develops, and promotes the art forms of film, television, and games. The organizations runs the annual British Academy Film Awards. Only British programming is accepted.

Cinema Tous Ecrans

http://www.cinema-tous-ecrans.com/

The Cinema Tous Ecrans (All Screens Film Festival) is an independent film and TV festival held in Geneva, Switzerland. There is an award category competition for International Web Series.

Digital Hollywood

http://www.digitalhollywood.com

Founded in 1990, this industry trade conference covers the fields of film, television, music, home video, cable, telecommunications, and computer industries. The event often has panels involving web television.

Emmy Awards

http://www.emmys.com/awards

This is *the* awards competition for television. The first Emmy Awards ceremony was on January 25, 1949. We often think of more traditional television series only winning Emmy awards, but web series have been winning awards. Here are a few examples.

- *The Lizzie Bennet Diaries* won a Creative Arts Emmy for Original Interactive Program in 2013.

- *Venice The Series* won a 2011 Daytime Emmy for Outstanding Special Class Short Format.

- Canadian web series *Guidestones* won the 2013 International Emmy Award for Best Digital Program: Fiction.

- Netflix has blurred the line of traditional television and political thriller; *House of Cards* only furthered that blur by being nominated for nine Primetime Emmys, winning two Creative Arts Emmys for Outstanding Casting for a Drama Series and Outstanding Cinematography for a Single Camera Series.

FirstGlance Film Festival (Hollywood)

http://firstglancefilms.com/
Founded in 1996, the FirstGlance Film Festival is a bi-coastal film event that takes place in Los Angeles and Philadelphia each year. The festival has screenings and awards for projects of various lengths and formats, including web series pilots. The festival also has VOD distribution opportunities for films.

The Geekie Awards

http://www.thegeekieawards.com/
I had the pleasure of being one of the judges for the Geekie Awards. It is an award show that (to quote them) "... presents the best indie-created, high production value, awe-inspiring geek-genre content, art, products and experiences in the world. We, as creators, have never found one show that covered all of our multi-faceted talents, and often, we've discovered that the rest of the world didn't take our work seriously because it was 'geeky.' So we created our own show to give indie 'geekmakers' a place to shine and be seen by leaders and experts in their respective industries."

They have a wide range of categories of awards including Best Short Film, Best Podcast, Best Tabletop Games, etc. But the category you are probably most interested in is their Best Web Series category. The first show was in 2013 and was streamed live with geek celebs like Seth Green (*Austin Powers*, *Buffy The Vampire Slayer*), Richard Hatch (*Battlestar*

Galactica), Chase Masterson (*Star Trek: Deep Space 9*), and many more. So if your web series has a geek slant then you should consider this award show. Not only could you win and be given an award by a geek celeb live online at a fun awards event show in LA, but the Geekie Awards also makes a point to feature each entry on their website, so you get a little extra exposure even if you don't win. This is unique to this show and provides another reason to submit your project.

Hollywood & Vine Film Festival

http://www.hollywoodvinefilmfestival.com/
Founded by *Hollywood & Vine* magazine, the Hollywood & Vine Film Festival (HVFF) is on a mission (in their words) "...to provide industry access to emerging content creators and to showcase their talent throughout the U.S. and in over 10 countries. Submission materials include media projects that have not yet been distributed through a mainstream outlet such as a studio, network or independent distributor." They have a wide range of categories including web series, feature films, short films, documentaries, music videos, TV pilots, scripts, trailers, and— a rarity in film festivals—sizzle reels and artists' reels.

International Press Academy Satellite Awards

http://www.pressacademy.com/
Each year since 1996, the International Press Academy (IPA), an association of professional entertainment journalists, has given out Satellite Awards for artistic excellence in the areas of Motion Pictures, Television, Radio, and New Media. The IPA was actually one of the first traditional organizations to recognize New Media.

Internet Week

http://www.internetweekny.com
Since 2008, Internet Week has been a quickly growing conference focusing on New York's web industry in various forms. There are conferences, speeches, parties, workshops, awards shows, and how-to sessions which will be of interest to web series creators.

ITVFest

http://www.itvfest.com/

Founded in 2006, the ITVFest (the Independent Television and Film Festival) is a festival for showcasing independently produced television shows, web series, multimedia content, and short films. Content creators in the festival range from new filmmakers to Emmy winners. The festival moved from Los Angeles to Dover, Vermont, in 2013. The festival on average receives 200–300 submissions each year, from which 30–40 selections are chosen. There are a number of individual success stories: web series sold to Sony and College Humor, NBC buying pilot scripts, writers hired onto *The Colbert Report*, pilots sold to Comedy Central. There are celebrity panels which in the past have included cast and crew from *Simpsons, House, Always Sunny, Reno 911, The Unit*, and other shows.

Motion Picture Sound Editors (Golden Reel Awards)

http://mpse.org/golden-reel-awards/

Since 1988, the Motion Picture Sound Editors has handed out annual Golden Reel Awards for various areas of sound editing: Dialogue and ADR, Effects and Foley, and Music.

New Media Film Festival

http://www.newmediafilmfestival.com

Since 2009, the New Media Film Festival has been an international festival based in Los Angeles that accepts new media entries across a variety of categories: web series, feature films, 3D shorts, LGBT, and more. The jury has included reps from Pixar, Fox, and others. Each festival has a networking lounge, red carpet press junket, 3D opening night screenings, awards ceremony, and more. There are panels that include experts in new media technology and film. Each entry is considered for screening at the festival with a competition for $45,000 in awards and for distribution.

New York Television Festival (NYTVF)

http://www.nytvf.com/

Founded in 2005, the NYTVF is a web series–heavy festival for professional material that is often independently produced. Their

Digital Day is a forum for discussions and screenings of web series. The festival also sponsors the Independent Pilot Competition which showcases original television pilots to industry executives. There are also parties, seminars, Premiere Week, Industry Day, and other events.

Producers Guild of America Awards

http://www.producersguildawards.com/
The Producers Guild of America hands out awards each year and web series can be submitted under the Outstanding Digital Series category. Some well-known past nominees include *The Guild*, *H+: The Digital Series*, *Video Game High School*, *The Lizzie Bennet Diaries*, and *Red vs. Blue*.

SAG Awards

http://www.sagawards.org/submissions
If your web series production was done under contract with the Screen Actors Guild, you could try submitting to the SAG Awards. Needless to say you'll be up against some tough competition.

Shorty Awards

http://shortyawards.com/
The Shorty Awards honor the best of social media content produced across Twitter, Facebook, Tumblr, YouTube, Instagram, Vine, and the rest of social media. Nominations are actually done via Twitter. So a grassroots social media movement could get your project nominated. During the 5th Annual Shorty Awards nomination process, more than 2 million tweet-nominations were sent out. After nominations are final, the Real-Time Academy of Short Form Arts & Sciences chooses the winners.

South By Southwest Festival (SXSW – Digital Domain film)

http://sxsw.com/film/sessions/digital-domain
Since 1987, the South By Southwest Festival has showcased film, music, and more in Austin, Texas. The Digital Domain part of the SXSW Film Conference was introduced in 2012 to focus on the constantly changing web environment. This section explores web series, interactive documentaries, apps, rich media projects, and much more. The SXSW has panels with marketers, creators, and industry leaders.

The Lovie Awards

http://lovieawards.eu/

The Lovie Awards' mission (in their words) "...is to recognize the unique and resonant nature of the European internet community – from Europe's top web and creative networks and content publishers to cultural and political organizations and bedroom bloggers."

The awards are named in honor of mathematician Ada Lovelace. As hinted in their mission, this European award show has a wide range of categories: Internet Video (which is why they made this list), Websites, Online Advertising, Mobile and Applications, and Social. It is considered Europe's alternative to the Webby Awards. If your web series is made in Europe then you may want to consider submitting.

Unofficial Google Plus Film Festival

http://www.ugpff.com and https://plus.google.com/+UnofficialGooglePlusFilmFestival

Founded by Adam J. Cohen in 2011, this film festival strives to showcase the best short films and web series by using the Google Plus Hangout technology.

"I was looking to make a world-class film festival experience available to filmmakers all over the world," Cohen told me. "In addition, I wanted to strengthen filmmaker communities by giving them reasons to get together in their home towns and celebrate film."

The festival takes place both online where you can watch the festival streaming live or at various real-world locations where you can attend panels. In 2013, the Unofficial Google Plus Film Festival teamed up with SnagFilms to provide filmmakers distribution beyond the dates of the festival, which includes a revenue share.

There are four main categories: Narrative Short Films, Animated Short Films, Documentary Short Films, and Web Series. Films must be 25 minutes or less in length. Each film is watched by a number of screeners and rated on a number of different categories. The scores are tallied and the top films are selected for each category. Industry experts then judge the winners.

Vidcon

http://www.vidcon.com

VidCon is (in their words) "..for people who love online video. Independent creators, enablers, viewers and supporters of all kinds. The ways that we entertain, educate, share, and communicate are being revolutionized." Created by YouTube heavyweights Hank and John Green (best known for their YouTube channel VlogBrothers), this conference is both an industry conference and a big party. The Anaheim Convention Center in Anaheim, California, has hosted all of the VidCons to date. If you have your own YouTube channel or show, then this could be a good fit for you. Not to say that it isn't welcoming to scripted web creators or other online talent, but it leans heavily toward YouTube creators who do vloggers and similar non-narrative structured videos.

The Webby Awards

https://entries.webbyawards.com/

The Webbys are one of the older internet-oriented awards, started in 1997. The awards are presented annually by The International Academy of Digital Arts and Sciences and include broad categories well beyond just web series. These categories have changed over the years. At the time of this writing their primary categories are Websites, Interactive Advertising and Media, Online Film and Video, Mobile and Apps, and Social.

Writers Guild of America (WGA) Awards

http://www.wga.org/wga-awards/submissions.aspx

If you have gotten this far in the book you should already know who the WGA are. It is possible to submit a web series to their awards under the TV-Radio-New Media Scripts, but to be eligible, it must have been written under the WGA MBA or under a bona fide collective bargaining agreement of the Writers Guild of Canada, Writers Guild of Great Britain, Irish Playwrights & Screenwriters Guild, or the New Zealand Writers Guild.

Conventions

Boston Comic Con

http://www.bostoncomiccon.com/
This Comic Con takes place in Boston, usually in August.

Dragon Con

http://filmfest.dragoncon.org/
Part of the Dragon Con convention in Atlanta is the Dragon Con Independent Film Festival. The festival is a combination of short and feature independent film screenings, panels, celebrity guests, discussions, etc. It leans heavily towards short films and feature films, but they do accept submissions for web series. If your web series is sci-fi, fantasy, horror, or geek comedy related then you may want to check out this festival.

Gen Con

http://www.gencon.com/host/filmcontest
As a self-professed gamer, I have always been a fan of Gen Con. But besides being the largest gaming convention in North America, it is also home to a film festival for feature films, short films, and web series. It is held every year in Indianapolis, Indiana. If you win for Best Film, Best Short, or Best Series you can win a cash award and a booth for next year. Failing that (starting 2014) you could win a certificate for Best Animated Film, Best Gamer Film, Best Documentary Film, Best Fantasy Film, Best Sci-Fi Film and Best Horror Film. There are also panels and events. If you think your web series fits these genres or could appeal to a gaming audience, then you should submit to them.

New York Comic Con

http://www.newyorkcomiccon.com/
New York Comic Con is a large convention that might provide you an opportunity at a booth, panel, or screening.

Phoenix Comicon

http://www.phoenixcomicon.com/

The Phoenix Comicon Film Festival accepts films and web series. They have "best of" awards and I know of many web series that have submitted to them over the years. Worth checking out if you have a web series that fits the genres they accept.

San Diego Comic-Con

http://www.comic-con.org/

This is the mother of all Comic Cons. There may be screenings or panel opportunities, especially if you team up with other web series creators.

Wonder Con

http://www.comic-con.org/wca

Another Comic Con, this one is held in Anaheim, California.

Now What?

You've been shown a wide range of festivals and award shows that you can submit to. Of course, the best way to decide which ones to submit to is by visiting their websites and perhaps even asking any other web series creators you know that have submitted to them. Another good way to figure out if an award show is a good fit for you is by seeing what type of series wins. If your show is like one of their winners, then that is a good sign you should try for them.

THAT'S A WRAP! NOW LET'S DO IT AGAIN.

Woohoo! You've premiered online with your first season. You are making the festival rounds and promoting awards and nominations. Hopefully you are keeping connected with your fanbase. You either loved the experience or hated it, but either way you finished a huge goal that many don't ever complete, much less start. But now what?

Defining Success

First off, you need to figure out if your first season was even a success. There are seven main Goals. Did you accomplish one of them or are on your way to doing so?

Goal 1: Making Lots of Money

Goal 2: Critical Success

Goal 3: Become a Traditional Movie

Goal 4: Become a Traditional TV Series

Goal 5: Picked Up by a Studio

Goal 6: Create New Career Opportunities

Goal 7: Telling Your Story, Your Way

There is no rule that you can't succeed in more than one goal or that it may take more than one season to accomplish one of them. But, luckily Goal 7 is almost a sure thing and is one of the most rewarding things about independent web series creation; creating the series you want, the way you want to.

What Can You Expect With a Season 2?

Now that you've finished Season 1, the question everyone will ask is if there will be a Season 2. Many web series don't do a Season 2, either because the show wasn't a big enough success or the show was such a success that it led to new opportunities that will attract fans of your series.

If your series did well, and if you creatively want to, give yourself a small break, then jump into Season 2. You will find that Season 2 will likely be easier, especially if Season 1 received any awards or drew any attention. Talented actors and crew will be easier to get. You'll have learned from mistakes and will be able to smooth out your workflow. And you will have media contacts now who know you, so getting new interviews will be much easier.

How to Build Momentum

When I say give yourself a break, I mean not too much of one. You'll want to start writing those scripts early on and try to have new episodes in time for the next cycle of your favorite award show or festival. Who is your favorite? Whichever one gave the most recognition and you enjoyed the most. That one or ones like it will be your target for next season, because you can be more confident they will make some kind of splash there with new episodes. You might even be able to premiere a new episode at the festival or arrange some kind of special panel if you've developed some kind of fanbase at it. For example, Zombie Orpheus Entertainment has few festivals and conventions that they hit every year, but Gen Con is always one of the big ones where they try to plan big events. So much so that for 2012 and 2013 they rented out an entire hall for screening ZOE productions and other series from other producers that have partnerships with ZOE. This is the kind of offline foothold you might be lucky enough to get. It may be a large festival or it may be a smaller hometown festival, but having an event to spring off of for future seasons is a great strategy, and a good way to push your team on a deadline that keeps momentum up for new seasons.

Is it Sustainable?

You have to be honest with yourself. How sustainable is your series? Hopefully you have asked yourself that question before you launch the first episode. I'm not just talking about if the concept has legs to run for years, but I also mean is it financially realistic for the long run? *The Guild* ran for six seasons with a total of 70 episodes. Of course those episodes are 3–12 minutes each, so not as impressive as traditional one-hour dramas that run for years, but even though the screen time is shorter the blood and sweat price was no less. Felicia Day worked hard to fund each season mostly independently and called in a lot of favors. Six seasons is a tremendous success for an indie, scripted web series. So before you plan on ten seasons with multiple one-hour episodes or something similarly crazy—because we are all trained to think of television that way—keep in mind that everyone is working for little money and their time is as important as yours.

Be realistic how sustainable your series is for everyone involved. Your goal is to keep it as simple as possible for the story you are trying to tell and keep a sustainable budget. If you are the creator of a series or one of the main team members, you know by now that it will consume much of your time and energy.

So, make sure you don't get too complex with your series: Save some of your concepts for when you hit it big and can pitch them to a studio or network. And make sure you really want to make more seasons. Don't do it just because it is expected; do it because you really want to.

Is Web Television for You?

You just finished your first season. Now, how do you feel? It may sound silly, but really take time to reflect on the experience. Not everyone is built to be a showrunner of a web series. It is a lot of work. In many ways it is more work than a feature and is without a doubt a longer commitment than a short film, which would normally require just a handful of days.

You may make the cycle of web series festivals and just not feel like you fit in. You may not really have stories you want to tell in a serial format. You may not be happy with the work level with the low potential pay versus a feature film which is a long shot, but could give a decent payday. Ask yourself is web television the medium you want to keep working in, or would you rather go into films or some other medium?

There is no shame here. Each of us has different stories we want to tell and each of us has different skill sets. Now that you've completed a season, use that experience to reflect and decide if web television is really for you. If not, save this book in case you change your mind in the future, and grab a new book on whatever medium you might want to do next (narrative feature film, short film, documentary, music videos, etc.) and start a new journey to blaze your path on.

Whatever you decide, you'll have picked up fantastic skills making your first series, made new contacts, and gotten your name out there.

Congratulations, You Are a Pioneer!

Whew, you did it. You read this entire book! You've learned the history of web television, the major organizations, the press contacts, how to market a web series, how to raise funds, been given lots of examples of different web series, received writing advice, and more.

This is the book I wish I had when I was making my first web series. This medium is the fastest growing out there and the rules are still being written. In the time it took me to write this book the number of web series festivals more than doubled, a US president decided to be a guest on a web series, and major studios started buying YouTube Multi-Channel Networks for hundreds of millions of dollars.

The web television world is a fast moving one, but with that dynamic energy and its challenges also comes the excitement of being a pioneer. Of being on the cutting edge of entertainment. I have no doubt in my mind that the next Hitchcock, Spielberg, Lucas, or Tarantino is out there currently working in web television. Could it be you? Go forth and find out. It is time to be a pioneer blazing your own path to success!

APPENDIX A

Resources

Here are some more excellent resources you will likely need in your journey to make your own web series.

Royalty-Free or Low Cost Music

Music can make or break a project. Ideally, I always get a music composer to create an original sound track. But if you just don't have the contacts or funds for that, or perhaps you are just looking for some quick music for a teaser, then check out these links for royalty-free or inexpensive music.

Audio Jungle (http://audiojungle.net)
Audio Micro Stock Library (http://www.audiomicro.com)
Audio Network (http://us.audionetwork.com)
ccMixter (http://www.ccmixter.org/)
Elias Music Library (http://www.eliasmusiclibrary.com/#home)
Free Music Archive (http://freemusicarchive.org)
Incompetech (http://incompetech.com/music/royalty-free)
PremiumBeat.com (http://www.premiumbeat.com)
Stock Music Boutique (http://stockmusicboutique.com)
SoundCloud (https://soundcloud.com)
StockMusic.com (http://www.stockmusic.com)
StockMusic.net (http://www.stockmusic.net)
Vimeo Music Store (http://vimeo.com/musicstore)

Free Software

We often think about how expensive hardware like cameras and lights are, but forget there are other costs like software, which could make for pricey post-production. Software can be an expensive price barrier, but don't let that stop you. You can get excellent discounts if you are a student. But failing that, there are still plenty of free or cheap options for software online (and I'm talking about the legal kind of options, just to be clear). They may not have all of the latest bells and whistles, but they have all of the tools you will need to make an independently produced web series.

For Writing....

Celtx

https://www.celtx.com

Celtx provides a low-cost option for scriptwriting software and it even has post-production tools that could be very helpful for you if you are working on a tight budget and need something to help with breaking down the script and doing callsheets. The basic software is free, but many of the best features will require a paid upgrade.

OpenOffice and Libre Office

https://www.openoffice.org and https://www.libreoffice.org

Can't afford Microsoft Office's software, but need something for writing documents or spreadsheets? No worries. OpenOffice and kissing cousin LibreOffice are excellent free options that work perfectly fine and give you more format options including saving the files as PDFs. Whether it be writing outlines, creating spreadsheets, or putting together presentations, these two can do it.

For Video Editing & Visual Effects....

Adobe Premiere Pro 2

In 2013 Adobe did something unexpected and released the video editing software Premiere Pro 2.0 online as freeware. So if you need basic editing software, this could be a valid option. It is a few versions behind (currently version 6 is out) so it can only do so much, but it may be all you need when you first start out.

Blender

http://www.blender.org/

Blender is a 3D graphics application released as free software under the GNU General Public License. You can use it for modeling, UV unwrapping, texturing, rigging, water simulations, skinning, animating, rendering, particle and other simulations, non-linear editing, compositing, and creating interactive 3D applications. A cool example of an indie production using Blender is the Seattle-made indie film *Project London*. With nearly no budget, it created more than 780 computer-generated effects for action sequences with huge robots in a futuristic setting using this free software and volunteer artists.

APPENDIX B

Aidan 5 Pilot Script

Aidan 5 has won a number of awards and tied Felicia Day's *The Guild* as the most nominated series at the 2013 International Academy of Web Television awards. I've had the pleasure of working with its creators on their second season and asked them if I could include one of their scripts to give you a sample in case you are new to scriptwriting. It is one of the more elaborate drama scripts you'll likely read from a web series, so it should be a good learning experience or at least some fun. Enjoy!

AIDAN 5 -- The Web Series

EPISODE #101
"The Rooftop"

Written By:
Tim Baldwin, John Jackson, Ben Bays

WHITE DRAFT June 4, 2009

The City, 2064

FADE IN:

EXT. TOP OF BUILDING — night

Civilian hovercraft and police cruisers streak across the night sky. A police siren wails in the distance. We see two figures standing on the roof of a tall building. There's a body to the side of them. One of them leans down to examine the body.

> AIDAN (V.O.)
> Another one down. This is the third time today I've seen my lifeless face.

Aidan turns the body over and stares at his own face. It is a CLONE, an exact duplicate of him. Aidan shakes his head. A card left on the body reads "You're next."

DISSOLVE TO:

INT. police office — earlier in day

The office is busy. Police officers and plain clothes detectives work at their desks.

> AIDAN (V.O.)
> My day started off normal.

Aidan enters through the main door and heads towards a coffee station on the other side of the main working area.

> AIDAN (V.O.)
> I guess in theory, a cloned detective can get more done...

He's immediately flanked on either side by a clone of himself, each one uniquely dressed.

> AIDAN (V.O.)
> Work around the clock, solve more cases...

                    AIDAN CLONE 1
Heard you demolished the lower east side
last night...

                    AIDAN CLONE 2
...where you were playing knight in
shining armor again.

                    AIDAN
You guys are just jealous you'll never
be me...

                    AIDAN CLONE 2
    Ouch...

                    AIDAN (V.O.)
...well, that's the theory.

A voice echoes across the hall.

                    LIEUTENANT (O.C.)
    Aidan!

THE LIEUTENANT enters and heads toward the three
Aidans, fuming.

                    AIDAN CLONES
    He means you.

Both clones promptly step aside as the Lieutenant
and Aidan arrive at the coffee station.

                    LIEUTENANT
You mind telling me why I've got a civil
lawsuit on my desk this morning?

                    AIDAN
        (pouring a cup)
If you saw the cigarette burns I saw...

                    LIEUTENANT
Detective, you put her husband's head
through six inches of concrete!

Aidan Clone 1 glances at Aidan 2 while moving his lips... six inches!

> AIDAN
> I'm sure the victim didn't mind.

> LIEUTENANT
> She's the one who initiated the lawsuit!

This stops Aidan short.

> AIDAN
> (more to himself)
> Why do they always protect those bastards?

Another one of Aidan's clones stops next to the Lieutenant.

> AIDAN CLONE 4
> Lieutenant, Detective Randal is ready for the Mayor's security briefing.

He hands the Lieutenant a folder, which he promptly begins signing.

> LIEUTENANT
> Even your damn surrogates know their place around here. Maybe you should take notes.

Aidan blows off the remark but exchanges glances with all three of his clones. He heads to the elevator. Doors close.

INT. 10th floor precinct — MOMENTS LATER

Aidan steps off the elevator and walks to his office.

INT. AIDAN'S OFFICE — CONTINUOUS

As he enters, Detective RILEY is waiting for him, sitting at his desk.

                         AIDAN
          What are you doing in here?

                         RILEY
          Covering for you. Heard you had a late
          night.

                         AIDAN
          Cigarette Man.

                         RILEY
          At it again, huh?

                         AIDAN
                    (staring out the window)
          That guy put her baby in the trash
          compactor and was threatening to turn it
          on when I showed up. After I... talked
          him down...

This comment draws a look from Riley. Aidan
acknowledges and continues.

                         AIDAN (CONT'D)
          I lifted that baby from the rotting
          garbage and she couldn't breathe. I
          wiped the sludge from her mouth and
          nostrils, and it started wailing the
          most beautiful sound I ever heard.

Suddenly the phone on Aidan's desk rings. Riley
answers.

                         RILEY
          Detective Aidan's office, this is
          Detective Riley.

A moment passes as she listens to the other end.
A grave look washes over her face, and tears form
in her eyes. Aidan notices.

                         RILEY (CONT'D)
                    (shocked)
          Thank you... we'll be right down.

                    AIDAN
              (V.O.)
    Illegal cloning leveled the playing
    field.

INT. Morgue table — CONTINUOUS

On a gurney lies a clone of Aidan, the sheet
pulled off of him. Surrounding the table is Riley,
the Lieutenant, and four other Aidans. They look
down at the clone. There is a small white card
with the body that reads "One down."

                    AIDAN
              (V.O.)
    It's just another corpse. At least,
    that's what I tell myself.

INT. POLICE STATION — NIGHT

The three Aidan clones are standing around a giant
video screen displaying a map of the city. As the
clones speak, they move points of lights around
the video screen with lightning-fast efficiency.
Aidan sits nearby watching them work like a coach
on the sidelines.

                 AIDAN CLONE 1
    He was found on 18th street, not six
    blocks from here...

                 AIDAN CLONE 2
    ...meaning there were twenty-seven
    possible security cameras covering the
    area...

                 AIDAN CLONE 4
    ...not forgetting possible alternate
    routes he could have taken from the
    station when he left the precinct last
    night...

                 AIDAN CLONE 1
    ...last person to see him alive was
    Hicks in cyber division...

                          AIDAN CLONE 2
          ...who is still compiling the data files
          from the security cameras to give us a
          better indication of who he may have met
          after he left the office...

                          AIDAN (V.O.)
          Getting cloned was part of the deal when
          I took this job.

FLASHBACK — POLICE OFFICE

Aidan is sitting across from an older police
officer, signing a large stack of paperwork.
Everything is hazy and bright.

Aidan signs on the bottom line.

FLASHBACK — INFINITY CORP. MEDICAL ROOM

Doctors in lab coats extract blood from Aidan's
arm. The syringe glows red.

                          AIDAN (V.O.)
          I couldn't help but feel like I was
          losing a part of myself.

FLASHBACK — INFINITY CORP. CLONING LAB

Scientists and technicians load Aidan's blood
into a cloning tank. Everything is still hazy and
bright. We can't make out all of the details,
but we get the picture. They start the cloning
process.

                          AIDAN (V.O.)
          The Feds capped the number of clones
          allowed from a single source at five.
          The only approved patent is owned and
          operated by Infinity Corporation.

Large human-sized vats of saline solution start to
spin.

               AIDAN (V.O.)
   Infinity's public face is that of a
   flawless track record.

Human forms start to take shape in the vats of
liquid.

               AIDAN (V.O.)
   But you'll never hear them mention that
   during the injection protocol, my 3rd
   clone suffered a massive brain aneurism
   and died instantly.

Electrical lights flash as the silhouetted form of
Aidan 3 suddenly jerks forward for a moment and
then subsides. The form floats lifeless behind the
glass.

               AIDAN (V.O.)
   I've often wondered what went through
   his mind in that brief moment of
   consciousness.

                              FADE TO:

INT. Aidan's APARTMENT — NIGHT

Aidan sits on the edge of his bed in a tiny
apartment crowded with unopened moving boxes. His
pager goes off. He looks down. It reads 911.

EXT. ALLEY — later

In a dirty alley is another Aidan clone, dead.
Aidan stands over him. Surrounding the crime scene
are a few other detectives. Riley comes up next
to him and looks at the card laying next to the
body. It reads "How Many Left?"

               AIDAN (V.O.)
   It's not like we were best friends, but
   I feel... like I should feel something.

We push in on him as his pager goes off again. We
push in on the lifeless face of the clone on the
ground. Aidan looks at the pager: 911.

                    AIDAN (V.O.)
     At least something more than what I feel
     now.

We push in on the dead Aidan's face...

                              FLASH TO:

EXT. Rooftop — back to scene 1

We're back at the rooftop, with Aidan looking
at his 3rd dead clone. He stands up, still not
facing the other figure.

                    OTHER FIGURE
          How does it make you feel?

                    AIDAN
     Alone. Like no one is watching my back.

                    OTHER FIGURE
          I don't feel anything at all.

We RACK FOCUS to reveal the other figure. It's
the final Clone Aidan. He has a gun pulled on
Aidan.

                    CLONE AIDAN
          I guess that's the difference between
          us...

Clone Aidan pulls the trigger and fires.

                    CLONE AIDAN
          I don't feel anything at all.

He stares down on the body.

                    CLONE AIDAN (V.O.)
          That's the fourth time I've seen my
          lifeless body today.

The clone walks off of the roof leaving Aidan to
die.

                              FADE OUT.

ABOUT THE AUTHOR

© 2014 Courtesy of Amarus He.

After attaining college degrees in Psychology and Computer Information Systems, Marx H. Pyle decided to pursue a dream he had since childhood — filmmaking. Leaving his home in Evansville, Indiana, Marx went to Vancouver Film School in Vancouver, British Columbia, to study film production. In Vancouver he worked on a wide range of projects, including short films, independent feature length films, documentaries, reality television and commercials. His roles in such projects have varied just as much.

Missing home, Marx returned to the Midwest, where he has worked on various award-winning film projects and does freelance work on television projects for a wide range of channels (CMT, MTV, Lifetime, Food Network, Travel Channel, etc.). He joined and later became a board member of the Indiana Filmmakers Network.

Starting in 2005, Marx has written on various entertainment news websites and enjoys doing in-depth interviews with writers, producers, directors, and actors. Since 2007, when he interviewed his first web series creator, Damian Kindler (*Sanctuary*), he has sought out successful web series creators to interview. Currently he produces and co-hosts the popular online radio show called *GenreTainment*. He also writes for the entertainment news website ScifiPulse, where he focuses heavily on web series and other entertainment on the Internet.

His passion for learning more about web series would lead him to creating his own, starting with his award-winning web series *Reality On Demand*. This led him to working on other web series productions: co-producer/co-director for *The Book of Dallas* (which premiered to over a million views), director of photography for the Hugo-nominated web series *Star Trek: Phase II*, and stunt coordinator for award-winning *Aidan 5*. He is a proud member of the International Academy of Web Television and was a judge for the 2014 IAWTV Awards and for the 2013 Geekie Awards. Marx has no plans to slow down with his work on web series and other forms of filmmaking.

How to Contact the Author

You can learn more about Marx Pyle and his projects by visiting him at http://MarxPyle.com

To reach him directly, write to MarxPyle@gmail.com

CONQUERING YOUTUBE
101 PRO VIDEO TIPS TO TAKE YOU TO THE TOP

JAY MILES

What you need to know to become a You-Tube Superstar and go from no views to thousands or even millions of views by creating videos that people want to see. Amazing tricks and insider secrets fill the pages of this easy, hands-on guide to producing professional-grade videos for the Web. Classroom-proven exercises based on professional experience provide a top resource for exploring and mastering everything from basic camera operations to lighting, editing, and special effects. For those who want to take their videos to the next level.

Conquering YouTube is designed as a fun, easy to read text. Walks any videographer — from a true amateur to an experienced filmmaker — through all the steps necessary to create exciting and memorable videos for the Web. In an easy-to-digest format, the book couples clear instructions and descriptions with shooting exercises designed to sharpen the eye, develop specific and useful skills, and solve common production problems.

"Forget YouTube... this book is a grade-A primer for anyone learning to shoot video, whether it's for the Internet or Sundance. Using straightforward, easy-to-read explanations and helpful photos, Jay Miles has created an indispensable handbook for any young filmmaker."

— Chad Gervich, writer/producer: *Wipeout, Reality Binge, Speeders, Foody Call*; author: *Small Screen, Big Picture: A Writer's Guide to the TV Business*

"Accomplished videographer, producer, and teacher Jay Miles helps the novice and experienced shooter shoot better. Whether you're a new or experienced camera operator, Jay Miles' Conquering YouTube *will improve your skills and productions. Everything you need to make videos and make 'em better. Jay Miles' decades of working as a professional videographer, producer, and teacher are expertly summarized in this easy-to-read book. You will make better videos. Highly recommended!"*

— Don Schwartz, *CineSource* Magazine

JAY MILES has worked in TV, video, film, and commercial production for nearly 20 years, including shows for NBC, ABC, FOX, the Discovery Channel, HGTV, Versus, and DirecTV. He has completed productions for businesses (The House of Blues, Cisco/Linksys), bands (Two Man Advantage, The Afro-Semitic Experience) and blogs (*On Frozen Blog, The Washington Post*). He has taught media at the college and high school levels for the past four years. This book, his first, combines the professional and practical tips that he has used on major shoots and the approaches that he has used to help numerous beginners reach for the stars with their own successful projects.

$26.95 · 235 PAGES · ORDER NUMBER 159RLS · ISBN 13:9781932907940

CREATE YOUR OWN TV SERIES
FOR THE INTERNET - 2ND EDITION

ROSS BROWN

A first of its kind, all-in-one guide to creating short-form TV series for the Internet. Written in a hip and entertaining style in the language of the cyber generation, this book guides the aspiring videomaker from an initial series idea through writing, production, and uploading and marketing a polished pilot and successive episodes of his or her own original Internet TV series.

"The definitive resource for anyone who has ever dreamed of making their own television series ... Create Your Own TV Series for the Internet is essential reading before you pick up the camera."

> — Stefan Blitz, editor-in-chief, Forces of Geek

"Ross Brown's book is a must-read for anyone thinking of making a Web series or for anyone who's already made one, but wants additional insight into the process. It's absorbing, informative, and a fun read."

> — Michael Ajakwe Jr., founder and executive director,
> LAWebfest

"Ross Brown's enormously informative and entertaining book is enriched by his insider chops as a network series showrunner, and by his years of inspiring students in university television courses. This book is clearly a must-read for anyone interested in creating a do-it-yourself web series. But in a larger sense, it also presents the tools for establishing the enduring concept, core characters, and story engines required of any television series, regardless of length, making it an invaluable resource for anyone aspiring to a small screen career."

> — Brad Buckner, consulting producer, Supernatural

ROSS BROWN has written for and produced some of the most successful TV series of all time, including The Cosby Show, Who's the Boss?, and Step By Step. He has created primetime series for ABC, CBS, and the WB. Brown teaches at Dodge College of Film and Media Arts at Chapman University, one of the nation's top film schools, where he created the groundbreaking "Byte-Sized Television" courses.

$26.95 · 264 PAGES · ORDER #202RLS · ISBN 9781615931682

THE MYTH OF MWP

In a dark time, a light bringer came along, leading the curious and the frustrated to clarity and empowerment. It took the well-guarded secrets out of the hands of the few and made them available to all. It spread a spirit of openness and creative freedom, and built a storehouse of knowledge dedicated to the betterment of the arts.

The essence of the Michael Wiese Productions (MWP) is empowering people who have the burning desire to express themselves creatively. We help them realize their dreams by putting the tools in their hands. We demystify the sometimes secretive worlds of screenwriting, directing, acting, producing, film financing, and other media crafts.

By doing so, we hope to bring forth a realization of 'conscious media' which we define as being positively charged, emphasizing hope and affirming positive values like trust, cooperation, self-empowerment, freedom, and love. Grounded in the deep roots of myth, it aims to be healing both for those who make the art and those who encounter it. It hopes to be transformative for people, opening doors to new possibilities and pulling back veils to reveal hidden worlds.

MWP has built a storehouse of knowledge unequaled in the world, for no other publisher has so many titles on the media arts. Please visit www.mwp.com where you will find many free resources and a 25% discount on our books. Sign up and become part of the wider creative community!

Onward and upward,

Michael Wiese
Publisher/Filmmaker